URBAN SURVIVAL

STREETWISE STRATEGIES FOR STAYING ALIVE

URBAN SURVIVAL
STREETWISE STRATEGIES FOR STAYING ALIVE

SELF-DEFENCE • TACTICAL DRIVING
TERRORISM • KIDNAP • FIRE SAFETY
HOME SECURITY • PRACTICAL FIRST AID
SITUATIONAL AWARENESS • PLANNING

BILL MATTOS

LORENZ BOOKS

This edition is published by Lorenz Books
an imprint of Anness Publishing Ltd
info@anness.com
www.lorenzbooks.com
www.annesspublishing.com

A CIP catalogue record for this book is available
from the British Library.

Publisher: Joanna Lorenz
Editorial Director: Helen Sudell
Designers: Nigel Partridge, Adelle Morris, Diane Pullen
Additional text: Bob Morrison (Survival in the Home and
    Surviving Terrorism and Conflict), Harry Cook (Self-defence
    in the Urban Jungle)
Photographers: Bill Mattos, Helen Metcalfe, Kiah Allen,
    Yazmin Dunne and Tim Gundry
Illustrators: Patrick Mulrey and Peter Bull Studios
Production Controller: Ben Worley

Contents

Introduction

When most of us hear the word "survival", we tend to think of extreme wilderness conditions; the Arctic wastes, sandy deserts or the jungle, to name but a few. These places are full of hardships, and they test human endurance to its very limits. Yet there is much more to survival than this. In today's world, the ability to assess the risks of your urban environment (this is what professionals call "situational awareness"), and to prepare for them mentally and physically, equips you to deal with those accidents or events that can transform a familiar place or journey into a frightening and dangerous situation. This preparation and knowledge, clarity of mind and a positive and pragmatic mental attitude are all essential if we are going to confront the many dangers and challenges of the modern world and have the confidence to tackle emergencies effectively.

MENTAL FORTITUDE

Over the years, researchers and counsellors have collaborated to collate data on why some people can survive a life-threatening situation when others in the same situation are overwhelmed. Often it is not the strongest or those with the best equipment who make it, although these things undoubtedly make a big difference. The data always seems to imply that the difference between living and dying lies in the mind. The power of the mind, the resilience of the human spirit, an unshakeable optimism and a readiness to deal with the matter at hand are the vital factors in a survival situation.

This mental fortitude can be practised, and its strength increased just as you might increase the power of your muscles at the gym. Some people naturally have these qualities in abundance, but not all. However, there are skills that can be learned to help

us achieve the necessary mental strength. Just as we can repeat movements, like the running action or biceps curl, to make our bodies physically fitter, so the same principle can also be applied to the mind. But as with getting our bodies fitter, we have to work at it and repeat the action to increase our psychological resilience.

Training the mind allows us to cope with situations that take us way beyond any mental or physical pain threshold we may have set ourselves, and that these mental skills, once learned, can be applied to all survival situations. It therefore makes sense to look at these now, at the start of this book, before you read on.

▼ *If a fire broke out in your home, would you know how to get everyone out safely? Using visualization to help you to anticipate escape scenarios will enable you to cope that much better in a live situation.*

▲ *Respect your surroundings in the city as much as you would in the wilderness, and know the dangers and resources around you.*

The two most important building blocks for your mental fortitude can be summed up in two words – visualization and attitude.

VISUALIZATION

This is not psychobabble or spiritual mumbo-jumbo. Visualization has long been relied upon by elite athletes to prepare the mind, and surprisingly, the body for the rigours of the challenge ahead. The idea is that by performing an imaginary mental rehearsal of action, we can train for it because a mere thought can produce a physical response and reinforce the neural pathways in the brain that enable us to access this procedure more quickly and accurately.

An example of this that we can experience right now is to imagine sucking on a slice of lemon. When we do that we get a rush of saliva to the mouth - some people might actually be able to taste the lemon - yet there is not an actual physical lemon in sight. Our minds have just induced a physical response to the thought. Remember though, that this doesn't work if you've never tasted a lemon. Visualizing something you've never actually experienced calls on bringing comparable experiences and transferable skills into the visualization process. Often we cannot replicate a real survival situation in order to practise, but we can use our minds to imagine it and rehearse how we will respond. Having done this, we radically alter our emotional response to it. When visualization is used like this, it's like watching a scary movie for the second time. The first time you saw it you jumped at the upsetting bits and had a subsequent stress response; perhaps your heart was racing, and you had butterflies in the stomach, or cried or felt physically ill in extreme cases. But the second or subsequent times you watched the movie you no longer jumped at the scary bits because you knew they were coming.

In this case, the stress and arousal begins before the event happens on the screen, but builds more slowly and doesn't get so heightened as to overwhelm you. You have flattened the curve. In a real-life situation, it's important to do this, because everyone has their limit at which panic and the "fight or flight" response kicks in, rendering competence and rational thought a thing of the past, and dramatically reducing the chances of success. You have to keep it below that threshold, and visualization and mental preparation are the keys. Fear is a natural and essentially useful emotion, but overwhelming fear must and can be avoided by having that mental rehearsal in the bag. We simply need to press the play button when the situation arises.

THE POWER OF VISUALIZATION

Perhaps one of the most powerful ways to use visualization is as a means of developing that eternal optimism and hardness of human spirit that is so vital for survival. It is also possibly the simplest form of visualization to develop, for all you really need to do is visualize that one thing that is worth living for.

We all have something to live for – something we love more than anything else. Maybe it would be to hold your child again, drive your car, watch your favourite football team win a home game…Whatever it may be you just have to visualize it using every sense in your body and imagine how amazing it will feel to do that again.

A friend of mine has recalled thinking, as things got extremely awkward one day, "I can't die now. I haven't said goodbye to anyone. I

▼ *A positive attitude, an ability to adapt and dig deep for inner strength are key in attack or emergency situations.*

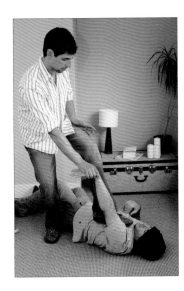

THE AIM OF THIS BOOK

This book aims to highlight many of the possible dangers that can arise within the urban environment and illustrate techniques and scenarios that may help in any given emergency situation. The book offers advice on self-defence techniques that can be learnt and adopted should the need arise. There is no guarantee that any of the physical self-defence techniques can ensure safety in every scenario.

Any self-defence action has to be taken using only 'reasonable' force, which is proportionate to the level of threat and then only if strictly necessary. The laws on the use of self-defence vary from country to country and it is important to stay within the law at all times.

▲ *Terrorism has changed the way in which we view our chances of survival and how we can prepare ourselves against the unexpected. An obvious example after 9/11 is airport and airline security.*

haven't even cleared my desk!" That mental commitment helps to give you the fortitude to carry on dealing with the matter at hand, however painful or terrifying it might be. It's not the only approach, but there is no doubt it works for a lot of people. Instead of thinking "Oh no! This hurts! I'm scared!", you can choose to think "I will survive because I need to say goodbye to my big sister/I can't leave my children/I'm not ready to die". Or any powerful emotion relevant to you.

ATTITUDE
The one element common to most survival scenarios is that we don't have a choice about being in these life-threatening situations. We can try to avoid them, but sometimes they are just unavoidable. For example, we have little chance of choosing not to be involved in a kidnapping, a terrorist attack or a natural disaster. The situation will usually be totally out of your control.

If this is the case, then it is vital to be able to recognize the things you can influence, rather than wasting precious time and energy worrying about things you cannot affect. You may not be able to change the dire situation you find yourself in, but you can choose the way you are looking at it.

"Choose your attitude" is the motto of solo Atlantic rower Debra Searle (nee Veal) MBE. Debra and her then husband Andrew took part in the

Ward Evans Atlantic Rowing Challenge at the end of 2001, but the sudden onset of her husband's phobia meant that he had to be rescued, leaving Debra to face the 5,000km/3,000-mile challenge alone. This she did with immense bravery, completing

▼ *Vigilance is the new buzzword of urban survival following a series terrorist attacks on public transport, entertainment venues and civic buildings around the world.*

her voyage in Barbados after 112 days and gaining universal respect.

For her, it was a case of picking an attitude every morning at sea and making sure it was a positive one. Negative attitudes had been banned on board the rowing boat. So optimism might be the attitude of the day, and a list of all the things there were to be optimistic about had to be formulated. The result was an upbeat feeling about what the day might bring, which is pretty surprising considering the situation. There is every excuse for a rotten attitude alone at sea in a small boat, lonely, scared and not sleeping for more than 20 minutes at a time for fear of capsizing, collision or attack by whales or sharks. The key to keeping going for Debra was refusing to dwell on how bad a given situation was, and choosing a positive attitude. Her transatlantic adventure became the talk of the media and an inspiration for other people battling against the odds in every area of life.

So as you read this book, don't just let the words and pictures flow around and past you. Practise visualizing yourself in the situation you are reading about, and imagine yourself responding as described. Rehearse the survival scenario now in the safety of your

home, or wherever you're reading it, just in case you ever have to face it for real. And remember – always choose your attitude.

▲ *The* Troika Transatlantic *was Debra Searle's home for 3½ months as she made a solo crossing of the Atlantic. She faced the mental challenge of survival alone at sea.*

SIX STEPS TO SURVIVAL

This book covers six major areas of urban survival: self-defence, travelling, survival in the home, terrorism and conflict, surviving acts of nature, and finally first aid. In Chapter One, we cover self-defence, drawing on martial arts techniques which will improve your fitness and confidence as well as helping you to defend yourself from attackers, whether armed or not.

In the second chapter the advice covers travel and getting home safely in an emergency situation; security; vehicle problems; and coping with disasters in air and on the sea.

In Chapter Three, safety in the home is covered. Home is often the safest place to be, but there's a lot to learn about making it that

way. Foil intruders and thieves, and find out how to deal with fire, leaks or flood and defend your home from unrest.

Chapter Four looks at terrorism, conflict and civil unrest. What would you do if you suddenly found yourself under attack? This leads on to the discussion of natural disasters in Chapter Five – volcanoes, lightning, flash floods, pandemics.

Finally, Chapter Six is a guide to emergency lifesaving first aid. Armed with the latest knowledge that will help you to manage casualties until medical help arrives, you will have the confidence to face any of the challenges described in this book, and have the skills and aptitude for urban survival.

▼ *We can learn survival skills such as self-defence for use out on the street when we find ourselves most vulnerable.*

Good mental health

We all recognize the benefits of physical training to keep our bodies in good shape, but most of us have never considered how important it is look after our mental health too. It's important to do so in order to be function well in your daily life, but especially vital when the going gets tough. Take a considered look at how you divide your time, and make sure you are devoting enough of it to the following things:

• Physical activity, even if it's quite gentle.
• Being outdoors for part of the day – fresh air and sunlight.
• Learning new skills, however simple.
• Relaxation – learn some relaxation techniques, such as deep breathing, if you need to.
• Meditation – still your mind for a few minutes a day
• Mindfulness – pay attention to whatever you are doing and remain curious.
• Socializing – interact with other people, friends, family, neighbours.
• Sleep – develop a regular sleep pattern and try to sleep for eight hours a night.

Be organized and tidy. Clutter actually affects your anxiety levels, sleep, and mental focus. It also makes you less productive and wastes way more time than tidying up does. Unhelpful coping and avoidance strategies include snacking on junk food and distractions like watching trash TV.

MENTAL HEALTH IN A CRISIS
If you are facing a medium- to long-term crisis, whether alone or with family, friends or colleagues, it is important to maintain your mental strength and effectiveness since these are key to your safety and survival. Try to keep on top of all the following.

Maintain your social network:
Staying in contact with people you trust is important for your mental wellbeing, as well as for the safety that

◄ *Being as prepared as possible will ease some of your worries. Make notes of what the priorities are and work your way through them.*

▶ *It is vital to keep yourself in really good shape to be prepared for any eventuality. In addition, there are positive mental health benefits from the release of endorphins associated with regular exercise.*

▲ *Keeping yourself busy is an excellent way to handle stressful situations. There will probably be practical things that you need to do; but keep yourself occupied with things that relax you when there are not.*

another pair of hands, another mind, or another set of eyes and ears can bring on a practical level. Think about ways to stay in touch with friends, family and neighbours, and maintain whatever communication channels are available in the circumstances.

Voice your concerns: It is OK to talk to those you trust about your worries. Bottling things up will only make matters worse. Talking issues through with people may actually help them as well. Don't limit this to your partner or close family. Use your social network to get as wide a perspective as possible.

Keep occupied with practical considerations: Figure out how you are going to get your essential household supplies and prioritise it. Liaise with your neighbours, family and friends to share the load, the risk or the cost. Continue to access any medical or psychological support that you need if it is still available. If that's the thing that gets dropped, everything will go downhill very quickly.

Manage your feelings: Concern about a challenging situation is completely normal. However, some people experience a debilitating degree of anxiety that can reduce their effectiveness. Try to focus on the things you can control. Prioritize all the points above. Think triage and make plans. Be careful to filter the information you access for the essential facts you need and don't fill your head with other people's fears or scare-mongering. In particular, don't constantly listen to news updates on

the crisis situation. Try to schedule yourself a regular time to check on the latest information, maybe morning and evening. Acknowledge that some things are beyond your control, but if you're feeling anxious or overwhelmed, try to reframe your unhelpful thoughts.

Look after your body as well as your mind: Your physical health has a huge impact on how you feel. In times of trouble, it can be that you fall into unhealthy patterns of behaviour. These can end up making you feel much worse. Try to eat well-balanced

▲ *Don't bottle up your fears and concerns. Talk, and listen, to friends, family, and even strangers if appropriate.*

healthy meals, drink plenty of water, and exercise daily. Even if you are physically healthy, your daily dose of exercise releases mood-enhancing endorphins and serotonin for the next 24hrs or so, which will help reduce any negative thoughts you have been harbouring. Avoid smoking nicotine, taking recreational drugs, or drinking alcohol as it is a well-known powerful depressant.

GOOD MENTAL HEALTH

The following are indicators of mental health being in good shape:
• You feel confident when faced with new situations or people.
• You feel optimistic.
• You are generally content.
• You do not punish yourself when things go wrong.
• You set goals.
• You have good self-esteem.

◄ *Take time to relax. Meditate, listen to music, read, but most importantly, give your body and mind enough time to recover and rebuild so that you are ready for whatever lies ahead.*

▲ *Make an effort to do everyday things –
family or group activities as well as spending
time alone: whatever reconnects you with
normality for even a short amount of time if
you are in a far from normal situation.*

**Carry On Doing Things You
Enjoy:** Unless that's unhealthy – see
previous page. If you are feeling low or
stressed out, you may stop doing things
you normally enjoy. Perhaps you'll feel
that the situation is too serious to
waste time doing a jigsaw puzzle, or
whatever. Make an effort, though. It
will help to keep your mind occupied,
which in turn will help to stop you
worrying all the time.

Take Time To Relax: Whatever you
normally do to relax will be doubly
important now. It will help with
difficult emotions and worries and
improve your general wellbeing.

Get Enough Sleep: Though it may
be hard to sleep when life seems to be
falling apart, it's really important. Try
to maintain a regular sleeping pattern
of going to bed and rising at the same
times and stick to good sleep practices:
no electronic devices an hour before
bedtime, and use relaxation techniques
or make yourself physically tired if you
need to.

There can be no greater challenge
to mental health than feeling that your
survival is in jeopardy. Even if you are
one of those people who is extremely
calm and pragmatic in the face of
danger, it is not unusual to face
debilitating mental health issues after
the danger has passed.

Common in these cases are Post
Traumatic Stress Disorder (PTSD) or,
in a sense, its polar opposite, a
dangerous inability to treat ordinary
everyday situations with the respect
they deserve. But for most people, a
threat to life brings with it an
immediate surge of stress, anxiety or
panic. If there is time to consider the

PTSD – POST TRAUMATIC STRESS DISORDER

PTSD is a condition that develops
after a traumatic experience. People
with PTSD often cannot stop
themselves from thinking about
their trauma and may be haunted
by flashbacks or nightmares. They
tend to feel isolated and irritable
and may exhibit intense feelings of
guilt and shame. They can have
trouble sleeping and find it difficult
to concentrate. Severe cases,
categorised as "Complex PTSD",
lead to additional symptoms. Adults
with complex PTSD may lose their
trust in people and disassociate
from others, have physical
symptoms like dizziness or
headaches and other pains, and
engage in risky behaviours like
alcohol or drug abuse. Suicidal
thoughts are also common.

danger, unhelpful thoughts intrude on
any attempt to think rationally. The
brain's executive function becomes
overwhelmed, leading to ADHD-type
behaviour and difficulty in prioritizing
actions and tasks effectively. Depression
may set in, leaving you with no energy
or motivation, which can be
dangerous. In a nutshell, you feel really
bad and perform even worse, just
when you needed to be on top of
your game and performing really well.

ADHD – ATTENTION-DEFICIT HYPERACTIVITY DISORDER

Attention-deficit symptoms include
not being able to listen or
concentrate, forgetfulness, making
careless mistakes, having a short
attention span and generally having
difficulty with the organization or
execution of even simple tasks.

Hyperactivity symptoms are
excessive physical movements like
fidgeting, difficulty in waiting (such
as interrupting), acting apparently
without thinking, and a lack of
awareness of danger.

ADHD had been believed to be a
developmental disorder that is
probably genetic in origin, i.e. that it
cannot develop in adults without the
behaviours having presented during
childhood. However, many health
experts now believe that diet and
environmental factors can play a role.
When the symptoms appear during
or after extreme stress or duress, it
may be a different mechanism from
the childhood condition but you still
have some or all of the symptoms.

The psychology of survival

WHAT IF?

We mentioned in the introduction that preparation, visualization, and attitude are the most important factors in determining how you will handle a difficult problem. You can work on your attitude, practise visualization, prepare physically (training) and practically (equipment and supplies) for any situation you read about in this book. The key to bringing these three concepts together is a way of thinking "What if?" What if your front tyre blew out? What if your accelerator stuck at full throttle? What if a mugger appears in front of you right now?

Thinking this way at all times can keep your brain active and alert, but it is also very close to being excessive in terms of anxiety or paranoia. Having said that, counsellors and support workers have noticed for decades that the people who survived natural disasters, made it out of a smoke-filled building and other dangerous situations where the odds were against them were overwhelmingly those who had the "What if?" mentality. So, as far as you can without making yourself overly anxious, try to follow the scout and girl guide motto "Be Prepared". Because if preparation starts in your head with "What if?" then visualization,

mental attitude, physical practice and gathering resources tend naturally to follow. If you live by this adage, you may find that confidence overcomes anxiety in many walks of life.

AWARENESS

Much has been made of the idea of mindfulness, being "present" or "in the moment". In the context of self-preservation, this translates to "awareness", of which there are essentially two kinds. Internal awareness is your understanding of how you are feeling – nervous, uneasy, or fired up - but also how high you can jump, how fast you can run, or how confident you can look. External awareness is what you notice and take

▲ A social situation or a threatening one? Either can have a positive or negative outcome, and it is your situational awareness and willingness to think "What if?" that can help in an unknown situation.

in from your surroundings. That guy - I definitely couldn't take him in a fight. That tunnel – only one exit at each end so if someone follows me in, I'm easily trapped by a person hiding at the other. The nearest exit door – if everyone else is panicking and milling about, how do I get to it?

◄ ►Stay alert when travelling. Look around you for potential threats and lifesaving exits alike. Scan the people around you for signs. Just by appearing to be aware, you will make yourself less of a favourable target. Dress and accessorise suitably; don't look out of place. If you don't seem to fit in, you can get noticed for the wrong reasons. If you have to run, you will dissappear into the crowd if you are dressed like everyone else. Reversible clothing is good – if they are following someone in a patterned shirt or jacket, they will not notice the person in a plain one, even if they have the same hair, legwear and footwear.

▲ *Don't wait until something is amiss before wondering where the exit is. Maintain awareness of your possible exits and the best routes to them, and have a plan for where you will wait or hide in the event that there is mass panic and a bottleneck at the exits.*

SIGHTLINES

These are the clear lines of sight from you to an object or person, but noticing them also helps you to know how to put something between you and a threat so that it can't reach you,

◀ *Think in advance about what would happen if your regular supplies were not available. Make sure you'd be covered for at least a week, better still a month.*

or perhaps even see you. Have you ever noticed how much calmer you feel when sitting with your back to a wall rather than a door or a window? It might be some kind of feng shui, but more likely it's a deep evolutionary instinct. Nothing is coming at you from a blind spot. You can see the entrances and the exits.

If someone appears in front of you, where would you go? Knowing where the exits are before something happens is a sensible procedure to adopt. In theatres, concert halls and cinemas it pays to sit on the end of an aisle so if you need to make a quick exit you are free to do so.

RECOGNIZE, ACKNOWLEDGE, SIDE-STEP

Once you have the "What if?" mindset to apply your attitude, visualization and preparation appropriately, and the habit of practising awareness of yourself, your environment, sightlines and exits, this will go a very long way towards keeping you safer than the person who just wanders through life.

However, the best way to deal with any threat can be summed up with these three words – recognize, acknowledge, sidestep. Recognize the threat, acknowledge that it exists but that it represents only one of the possible outcomes of the scenario, and finally taken action to sidestep it – in other words to circumvent that undesirable outcome. It's worth reading that last sentence back a few times, in order really to absorb it and adopt it as your way of being.

We can break down the general types of survival scenarios into two main concerns:

Direct threats to our wellbeing: Some of the most common threats include attack, robbery, poisoning, fire or drowning – that sort of thing. The survivability of these situations is dramatically improved by being prepared – mentally and through physical training.

Removal of accustomed elements of our lives: Access to money or the food supply chain, water supply, communications/technology, safe air quality, or all of the above. You really only have to remove one thing – like toilet roll, or pasta, and people start to behave quite obnoxiously. Remove something like fuel, and significant aggression boils over almost immediately. So what's the solution? The best way to remove yourself from the stress and danger of that aggression is to avoid being in that line for the pump, or the supermarket, or whatever. Which means being prepared by having surplus resources before disaster strikes, so that you don't have to be the one queuing for the last generator, for instance.

BUY YOURSELF SOME TIME WITH TRIAGE

Now, there's one concept that is very useful in dangerous situations if you can train your brain to use it. It's called triage. The concept of triage exists in many walks of life, but surprisingly few people are attuned to using it as their go-to strategy for all situations, whether trivial or potentially deadly. Medical operatives use it to decide what order to do things in, and so do combat soldiers, though their professional intentions are very different. In simple terms, some things need to be addressed immediately, some others after that, and some things not at all. In the medical sphere, triage could be defined as follows: "The assignment of degrees of urgency to wounds or illnesses to decide the order of treatment of a number of patients or casualties."

Clearly, it makes little sense to treat people in the order they turned up at an emergency department. The first person in line might have simply stubbed their toe, but the next one might have actually stopped breathing. So the patients/victims of attack should be categorized accordingly. When the concept was first used by the French medical operatives during the Napoleonic Wars, they were grouped like this: "Those who are likely to live, regardless of what care they receive. Those who are unlikely to live, regardless of what care they receive. Those for whom immediate care may make a positive difference in the outcome."

The final group would be treated first if personnel were limited, irrespective of other considerations. It's worth noting that modern medical triage typically uses a far more

complex model based on algorithms using scores derived from a quantitative physiological assessment. But the original, primitive model is still of use if you are the first on the scene and have multiple casualties to consider.

The fighting version of triage works along the same principles. If multiple threats are presenting themselves, there's not much point in asking them to form an orderly line. Quickly recognize the severity of the threats and deal with the most urgent or pressing one first. If one man is shouting and waving a shovel at you but some distance behind him another is pointing a gun, the best advice is to take out the shooter first if possible.

You may think that all of this is paranoia and bad for one's mental

▲ Mass vandalism and looting takes place all too easily when life goes wrong in an urban environment. You should already have a plan in place to protect your property and your friends and family, or to "bug out" if the safest place to be is out of town.

health. But being ready, trained, and prepared for whatever life throws at you is going to make you confident and content. Knowing what to do in a crisis is like having food in the house and gas in the tank, so there are fewer practical problems to worry about.

◄ Queues at the pumps occur even in the event of a predicted price rise. It will be so much worse if the supply of fuel is limited. Storing fuel in large quantities at home is not safe or practical, but a full tank makes for considerable peace of mind.

► Bullying and gang behaviour often rely on weight of numbers. It's best avoided by being inconspicuous – the "grey" man or woman – but being good at making a break for it is pretty handy too.

SELF-DEFENCE IN THE URBAN JUNGLE

There are two key factors in surviving the hazards of modern urban life. One is to develop an awareness of your environment, establishing good habits in your daily routines and using common sense to minimize risks – for instance, avoiding a deserted underpass in which all the lights have been broken. The second basic rule of survival is that if you have to rely on self-defence advanced preparation will prevent a poor performance. In other words, success depends on correct mental and physical training.

Identifying the risk of attack

There are places in the urban landscape that it's obviously best to avoid at certain times, but if you have to be alone in a deserted area you should carry an alarm or a makeshift weapon such as an umbrella or dog lead. Sensible footwear is vital – don't wear shoes that will slip off or cause you to stumble if you need to run.

Prevention is better than cure, but if you do have to resort to self-defence remember that in potentially violent situations stress causes the body to release adrenaline, preparing you for

flight or fight. However, this can make your movements less precise. It is only through training in a realistic way that you can learn to respond effectively when faced with danger.

The best way to develop effective skills is to join a martial arts school that concentrates on teaching methods of self-defence rather than developing competitors for sporting events. You need realistic training based on a genuine understanding of the demands of actual fighting, rather than visually impressive sports-based techniques.

AGGRESSIVE BEHAVIOUR

People are creatures of habit and in stressful situations habitual actions and movements tend to dominate. This is true of both attackers and defenders, and surveys of attacks show that various forms of aggressive behaviour can be identified and predicted.

Human predators are not that different from other hunters. Tactics used by aggressors, such as the use of stealth and surprise to isolate and then overpower a victim, often reflect the hunting habits of wild animals.

WHERE TO BE ON YOUR GUARD

▲ *In large car parks, numerous pillars and poorly lit areas make perfect cover for potential attackers, so maintain awareness in such places at all times, especially if they are deserted.*

▲ *When you are facing a cash machine it's hard to know what's going on behind. Look around whenever possible, and put cash into an inside pocket. Putting cash inside a handbag will make you an easier target.*

▲ *In a queue it's normal to allow strangers closer proximity than usual. It is best to hold something in your hand, such as a rolled-up newspaper. Drunks can be a particular problem here.*

▲ *Pickpockets and gropers are the usual problems on public transport. Keep valuables in an inside pocket, ideally zipped. As for gropers, the best tactic is to shout to draw attention to them.*

▲ *A poorly lit, deserted underpass can be dangerous as there are few escape routes. If you must use it stay close to one wall and check around corners before you turn. Use your eyes and ears.*

▲ *If you have to stop at lights in an unsafe area, keep the car doors locked and windows up. Look out for anyone approaching the car, and for missiles that could be used to smash a window.*

Attacks on men

Aggressive males often single out another man as a victim, sometimes seemingly for no reason. The classic "What you lookin' at?" opening gambit, or a hard shove with the shoulder when passing by on the street, or in a crowded bar, happens all too often. Thankfully, this usually gives us a few moments to prepare for the violence that is likely to follow. But by far the best approach is if we can avoid that playing out.

DON'T LOOK LIKE A TARGET

An overly aggressive person is usually a coward with self-esteem issues. They are unlikely to pick on someone who is calm and confident but not cocky, is making no particular statement (being the "grey" man), and appears to be able to look after themselves without presenting a challenge to rise to.

Physical fitness, therefore, as well as posture, dressing in an unostentatious manner, and having confident eye contact without staring are all attributes and behaviours that put you at less risk of being singled out. Try not to look afraid or uncomfortable.

DON'T ESCALATE

Whatever he says, don't respond in a confrontational manner. Remain calm and don't appear to prepare for violence. Respond to any conversation in

neutral, non-confrontational terms without ignoring him. Believe that there is going to be a peaceful outcome.

TRAINING IS KEY

If you are confident in your own physicality and have some training in self-defence or martial arts, you will feel ready to react competently without thinking, and that confidence will show. That alone is usually enough to stop someone from picking on you. Not just fighters and athletes, but dancers and models too are rarely selected as random victims simply because their body language exudes confidence and they feel less of an easy target to most attackers.

BUT WHAT IF IT DOES HAPPEN?

The three most likely scenarios in an unprovoked attack on a male all feature a punch to the head. The best practice in these situations is to recognize that an attack is imminent and run off before it happens, if that is achievable. But if not, the secret is to react immediately as the aggressor throws the punch (see overleaf). Hesitate and you will have been hit.

◀ *If the aggression is directed at you, the best course of action is to placate. Don't escalate. Be confident and reassuring while internally preparing to flee or fight.*

▲ *We've all seen groups of men unexpectedly explode into violence. It's not always apparent that it's going to happen or why. Situational awareness is a key skill in this scenario.*

COMMON ATTACKS ON MEN

Studies show that when both assailant and victim are men, the ten most common forms of attack, in order of frequency, are:

1 A push to the chest followed by a punch to the head.
2 A swinging punch to the head.
3 A grab to the front clothing, one-handed, followed by a punch to the head.
4 A grab to the clothing with two hands, followed by a head butt.
5 A grab to the front clothing with two hands, followed by a knee to the groin.
6 A bottle or glass to the head.
7 A lashing kick to the groin or lower legs.
8 A broken bottle or glass jabbed into the face.
9 A slash with a knife, usually a short-bladed lock knife or kitchen utility knife. (Hunting/combat-type knives tend to be used in gang violence and sexual assaults.)
10 A grappling-style head lock.

A TYPICAL ATTACK ON A MALE VICTIM

1 The attacker moves in close and attempts to intimidate his opponent by aggressive, loud, insulting language. Often a blank stare will accompany the use of threatening words and gestures.

2 The attacker pushes both hands into the chest, causing the victim to lose balance. He will usually try to push his victim over a chair or other object to increase the effectiveness of the attack.

3 The attacker next grabs his victim by the lapels and pushes him backwards again. By taking control of the victim's balance in this way he is making him vulnerable to further attack.

4 The attacker, now in full control, escalates the attack by delivering a blow to the victim's head with a bottle or other heavy object.

DEFENDING A PUNCH TO THE HEAD

When defending yourself against a blow to the head you need to act fast. You are aiming to deflect his initial punch and turn the attack onto your attacker. It doesn't really matter if the punch is a straight one, an uppercut or a swinging punch (a hook). What matters is to see which arm it is coming from, and respond as follows.

1 Bring both hands up to cover your face, like a boxer. On the side that the punch is being thrown at you, keep the elbow up and out. The other arm can do most of the job of protecting your face.

2 As the fist approaches, drop your elbow and hand over the punching arm and rotate your body away as shown. Keep forcing his arm down with yours.

3 Even out the weight on both of your legs and throw the best punch you can at his face or throat with your free hand. The throat is better, but if he is shorter or his chin is down, this may not be possible. A punch to the face is more effective than hitting his collar bone which will hurt you a lot and him not at all!

4 Follow the punch through with all your weight so that he overbalances even if your punch wasn't decisive. At this point, you decide whether to restrain him with the arm you have already trapped, or take the opportunity to run. Practice this with a friend, over and over, on both sides. It will quickly become second nature.

Attacks on women

There are a number of reasons why a woman might be attacked. As well as the risk of a sexual attack, a woman could be attacked by a thief intent on taking something valuable, such as a mobile phone or a purse. In these circumstances it is not worth risking your health; let the thief take what they want and escape as quickly as possible. Only fight when the attack is directed at you rather than your property.

SEXUAL ASSAULTS

While strangers may seem to be the greatest threat, statistics prove that this is not the case. In fact most rapes occur in the home: 32 per cent of rape victims are attacked by their partners and another 53 per cent by perpetrators known to them.

From a self-defence point of view this means that the natural caution exercised among strangers is relaxed when in the company of friends, so reducing the opportunity for a fast, decisive response. However, it is important to react positively when a situation changes from one of normal affection or social interaction. Rape is an act of violence intended to degrade and humiliate the victim, and in police

▼ *Use your eyes to continuously scan for potential attackers or areas where an attack might come from. Stay away from dark doorways where an attacker could hide.*

interviews rapists often report that they commit the act as much for a sense of power and violence as for sex.

Submission to the rapist's demands is often thought of as a way to minimize the intensity of the attack, but in fact it may serve to encourage the attacker, who rationalizes that the victim is actually enjoying the activity and is, in fact, "asking for it".

The emotional effect of rape can include eating disorders, sleeping disorders, agoraphobia, depression, suicide attempts and sexual difficulties.

On pages 43 to 45 we cover other sexual assault issues including typical strategies employed by rapists. We also offer advice on how to fend off sexual attackers in various street situations.

▲ *Badly lit car parks are high-risk areas for attacks. Always stay alert when approaching your vehicle and hold your keys ready in your dominant hand as a possible weapon.*

COMMON ATTACKS ON WOMEN

According to police records, these are the five most common forms of attack used by men against women and girls:

1 The attacker approaches the victim displaying a weapon as a threat. The weapon is then hidden and the victim is led away, often by the attacker holding the victim's right upper arm.

2 The attacker pounces from behind, grabs the victim's head or neck in a lock and drags the victim away to a quiet place, often bushes or a deserted lane.

3 As with 2 above but the victim is grabbed around the waist and carried or dragged away.

4 The attacker pins the victim to a wall with a throat grab (often using the left hand). He issues a threat as in 1, and leads the victim away.

5 The attacker approaches from behind, grabs the victim's hair with his left hand and drags her away to a quiet place.

A TYPICAL ATTACK ON A FEMALE VICTIM

1 The attacker grabs the woman's right arm with his left hand. This initial assault is often accompanied by threatening instructions intended to frighten the victim into compliance.

2 In this case the threat is reinforced by the attacker brandishing a knife.

3 The knife might be partially hidden by being placed along the attacker's forearm. However, the victim can see it clearly, especially if the attacker pulls her in towards the blade.

DOMESTIC VIOLENCE

The victims of domestic violence, which accounts for almost a quarter of all the violent crime reported, are most likely to be women and children. Weapons are less likely to feature in domestic attacks: the victim is more likely to be injured from repeated blows with the hands and feet as well as being thrown into walls and furniture. Attempts at strangulation may also feature in this kind of situation.

Characteristically, this kind of attack is not a single incident, and on average a woman will suffer 35 attacks from her partner before reporting the violence to the police. Domestic crime is the most under-reported type of violent crime, with about two-thirds of cases never coming to the authorities' attention.

Learning some basic survival strategies may minimize the chance of attack. On the physical level the ability to fight back will minimize the effects of an attack and may dissuade the attacker from using violence. Training can develop a level of self-esteem improving the victim's view of the world.

PERSONAL ALARMS

For well over a hundred years police officers carried the simplest form of personal alarm, a whistle, which could be heard over surprisingly long distances. Three strong blasts on it would bring speedy assistance.

Tiny modern key-ring whistles make useful personal alarms, but these days the more hi-tech, high-decibel, battery-powered alarm is more useful to carry in a handbag or pocket. They emit a sound louder than that of a shotgun, and just above the pain threshold. The most practical type has

▲ *This tiny high-pitch siren alarm also has a built-in torch.*

a wrist cord connected to a small pin which, when sharply tugged free, allows a spring-loaded contact to complete an electrical circuit, triggering an ear-splitting siren. The second type, which may be little larger than a lipstick, is activated by pressing a button. This type of alarm is more discreet to carry in a pocket or bag, but it is just as effective.

◀ *A personal alarm can be clipped to a bag or belt hook and activated quickly if an attacker pounces.*

Effective first blows

If you are being attacked by someone who is physically bigger and stronger than you it is vital that you act quickly and decisively. The only thing on your side is the element of surprise. Without doubt, the first blow should be decisive, allowing you to escape as quickly as possible. However, a number of factors could limit the effectiveness of your initial strike. The attacker may have been drinking alcohol or taking drugs, which will dull his response to pain. He may be wearing heavy clothing that absorbs some of the force of your blows, or your strike may be inaccurate. It is therefore important to follow up as quickly as possible with a number of blows, all intended to cause as much pain and disorientation as possible. Aim at the eyes, groin, joints and other vulnerable parts. Below are some useful first strike techniques that are worth learning. Train with a partner and repeat the moves until they become second nature in order to react quickly. If the attacker backs away, run towards somewhere safe.

ELBOW STRIKE

1 Close in, an elbow strike can cause a lot of pain. In training, drive the elbow round and into the focus pad, aiming to land with the point of the elbow. Pull the other hand back to rotate the waist and simulate pulling an attacker into the strike.

2 The strike leaves the attacker's groin area open for a follow-up kick or knee attack. Never rely on one technique – be ready to exploit any weakness or hesitation on the attacker's part. Your survival may depend on this, especially if the attacker is bigger than you.

HAND SLAP

1 An open hand slap inflicts pain and shock. In training, focus on using the hand like a whip and slap down or sideways, hitting with the palm and not the fingers. Keeping the wrist a little loose gives a whiplash effect.

2 If the slap is aimed at the neck, try to hit in and slightly downwards to damage the throat. The best target for this kind of strike is the eyes. An assailant will almost certainly lift the hands to the face if the eyes have been heavily slapped. Take advantage of this to kick the attacker's groin or knees.

ROUNDHOUSE KICK

1 The roundhouse kick makes use of the whipping motion of the hips and the supporting leg. Use your instep to hit the groin, knees or thigh as hard as you can. With a lot of training this technique can even be used against the head, but in general it is safer to select a target from the waist downwards.

2 A very effective way to use a roundhouse kick is to strike against the back of an attacker's knee. As well as causing pain and slowing him down there is a strong possibility that this strike will catch him off balance and cause him to stumble and fall. If this happens follow up your kick with a stamp to the ankle or groin.

KNEE JERK

1 The knee is a very effective weapon, and is often used when an attacker has seized you and pulled you close. The groin is a natural target, but many men will reflexively pull back if they sense an attack coming. By driving upwards it is often possible to hit the solar plexus. Other targets include the kidneys and the large muscles on the thighs. Try to augment the strike by gouging the eyes or biting the ear.

GROIN KICK

1 A direct kick to the groin can drain an attacker of strength and aggression. Use the knee like a hinge and snap the lower leg directly to the target. When practising this move, drive the kick upwards into the focus pad to develop maximum power and penetration. A male attacker who is kicked hard in the groin will usually bend forwards, holding his groin, leaving the eyes, throat and neck exposed to striking.

LEARNING TO PUNCH

1 Practise with a focus pad to develop accuracy and impact. Hit with the big knuckles, keeping the wrist straight, and drive the fist in a straight line, as if you were trying to break an attacker's nose or jaw. Keep your balance and use your waist and hips to add drive to the blow, hitting through the target.

2 When you apply the punch, your intent should be to hit the fleshy parts rather than the bones, which could damage your hand. A fairly light punch to the throat will cause breathing problems to any attacker, but be careful in training as the neck and throat are very vulnerable to blows.

Improving your physical fitness

In a self-defence situation it is the training not only of the body but also of the mind and spirit that can give you an advantage.

TRAINING FOR IMPACT

Your strength and stamina can be improved by correct weight training, and the accuracy and impact of your strikes can be developed by hitting a target. It is best to train for impact without gloves as it is unlikely you will be wearing any protection on your hands if you are attacked. At first hit lightly, aiming for accuracy, but as you become used to the feeling of hitting you can increase the intensity of your blows. Learn to hit as hard as you can. If you ever have to fight for your life against a stronger, heavier opponent you may have only one opportunity to land a decisive strike. Learn how to do it properly (see pages 24–25).

By adapting to the stresses of training you are also improving your ability to face the shock of physical confrontation: without becoming masochistic about it, look on the knocks and bruises you receive in the gym as a good investment.

TRAINING WITH A PARTNER

If you train alone, a punch bag is a very useful tool to improve your striking skills, but training is more productive and fun if you have a partner. If you join a martial arts school you will have a ready supply of training partners, but you may be able to recruit a friend or relative who also wants to develop some self-defence skills.

A training partner is very useful if you train with a pair of specialized pads worn on the hands, usually known as focus pads or hook-and-jab pads. By moving the pads around, your partner can simulate an attacker moving in a

▶ *Rotational core strength is also essential. This exercise alternates bringing your opposite knee and elbow together. For maximum effect, try not to drop your straight leg onto the mat.*

random way, and you can learn how to hit a moving target. It is very important when training with a partner to hold back a little on the degree of power used in strikes, locks and chokes. It is very easy to injure someone by mistake through over-enthusiasm or clumsiness. Begin slowly, adding power and speed as your levels of coordination and timing improve.

THE RIGHT TYPE OF EXERCISE

Fighting is exhausting. That's why most scuffles or brawls last only a matter of seconds. Physical fitness and being accustomed to high-intensity activity is, therefore, one of the biggest advantages you could bring to a fight situation.

Cardiovascular-conditioning is necessary to build up stamina and the ability to move quickly. Running for long periods outside or on a machine

▲ *Core (abdominal) strength is vital if you're going to deliver the power of your arms and legs. Top-down/bottom-up strength can be developed safely with this "crunching" movement, repeatedly bringing elbows and knees together from a lying position.*

in the gym is a good way to develop stamina. However, remember that you also need to be able to run fast over short distances when fleeing an attack, so mix it up with sprints of up to thirty seconds at 100% effort. Hill sprint interval training, sprinting 30 seconds up a hill and descending more slowly, is better still. Repeat up to five times per session.

The box jump is very useful for developing explosive (plyometric) leg strength. Start small, performing about ten repetitions each session, and

▲ *You can achieve a rowing (pulling) action with this suspension trainer, but equally well with stretch bands, face down with dumbbells, or simply by lying under a table and pulling yourself up on the edge of it.*

▲ *The chest press (bench press) is your go-to workout for pushing and punching. This can be done at home with dumbbells or improvised with other household objects.*

▲ *Any exercise that you can do with a machine or with free weights can be simulated with stretch bands (resistance bands), with a little imagination.*

increase the height incrementally week on week.

Upper body strength is also essential. By using dumbells, a barbell or a rowing machine, grip strength can be improved, and the pulling action of rowing duplicates the movements used in grabbing an attacker's hair or clothes.

The bench press develops strength in the arms, chest and shoulders. Train as heavily as possible – the increase of strength not stamina is the intent. Try to push the bar up as quickly as you can, but lower it slowly, taking 3–4 seconds for the descending or "eccentric" part of the exercise.

The "pec deck", a piece of equipment found in many gymnasiums, is a useful way of training the muscles of the chest and shoulders. However, the same effect can be gained using dumbells or improvized weights in a prone position. Choose the correct weight so that you can perform at least six repetitions but not more than ten. Rest, and repeat four times.

▶ *Simple bodyweight exercises like the press-up (push-up) can be every bit as useful as using a range of gym equipment. If it's too hard to perform on the floor, try using the stairs to get a more upright angle, which makes it more achievable.*

WEIGHT TRAINING

The easiest way to become physically strong is to join a weight training gym. If you are a total beginner join a class to learn how to do the exercises correctly and safely. As you gain experience you may want to train at home. As well as barbells and dumbbells you can try lifting heavy things such as large stones, bags of sand, buckets of water or car tyres.

▶ *Sprinting a short distance uphill and jogging back down several times over is good practice for making a quick getaway. Don't forget to train over longer distances too, to build up stamina.*

Self-defence training

The best way to defend yourself is by attending a self-defence course at your local gym or leisure centre, or by joining a club where the skills you learn can be used in a scenario where you are forced to defend yourself.

Recent developments in combat sport such as MMA (Mixed Martial Arts) and UFC (Ultimate Fighting Championship) have shown that some traditional methods work much better than others when in hand-to-hand combat. While all of the following traditional disciplines will be extremely useful and render you a much more difficult target than an untrained person, it has been shown that a combination of Jiu-Jitsu type throws and holds, a good skillset in kicking and punching, combined with knowing where to hit for maximum damage will be many times more effective. These strikes are rarely allowed in any "sport" discipline.

MARTIAL ARTS FOR SELF-DEFENCE

Judo is a very popular combat sport. Training is based on grappling and makes extensive use of throws and ground fighting. Since its introduction into the Olympics, the stress in training has been towards competition skills, but its intensity means that the techniques can be most effective in a self-defence

▲ *Jiu-Jitsu and Aikido are Japanese fighting arts that utilize gripping and grappling as well as striking and use of traditional weapons like knives and sticks. As such they are well suited to violent situations.*

situation. Being thrown hard into a wall, for example, will deter most attackers.

Aikido is another Japanese martial art. It makes use of circular movements, which are designed to intercept an attack, blend with the movement and throw the attacker. Advanced training in Aikido involves training with weapons such as the jo (a 1.27m/4.2ft wooden staff). In a real self-defence situation, these techniques can be applied to everyday implements such as walking sticks or umbrellas.

Judo and Aikido both have their

▲ *Karate is a martial art primarily concerned with striking. Its punching and kicking forms are extremely powerful, but you can train without any actual contact, which appeals more to some students.*

origins in the ancient fighting system of Jiu-Jitsu. Since this martial art was originally developed by and for the samurai, it is more suitable for life or death combat situations. All three are often taught in a very traditional setting where discipline is sacred. Jiu-Jitsu itself has enjoyed something of a return to popularity in recent decades and now focuses more on the ground fighting tactics to subdue an opponent.

Brazilian Jiu-Jitsu is a modern incarnation of the discipline that is extremely popular around the world. It is primarily seen as a sport with a major focus on grappling skills.

Karate-do is primarily a striking art, which concentrates on developing powerful punches, strikes and kicks. Some styles also make use of close-range knee and elbow strikes, throws and locks. It should be noted that many clubs train non-contact or light contact, which is perhaps not the best practise for real-world fighting. Tae Kwon Do is the Korean version of karate, and specializes in kicking methods.

◄ *Judo is essentially Jiu-Jitsu distilled into a formal sport, but that doesn't make it impractical. The grappling holds and throws are very effective in a tussle.*

▲ *Kick boxing is a good sport for anyone wanting to keep fit, but the punches and kicks you learn are among the most effective in a street fight.*

The term "Kung-fu" covers a wide range of Chinese martial arts. Some, such as Tai Chi Chuan and Qigong, are concerned mostly with health, while others such as the Wing Chun and Shaolin styles are traditionally taught as combat methods.

WESTERN FIGHTING SYSTEMS
Wrestling is a combat sport featuring grappling, and groundwork clinches, throws, holds and joint-locks. It is perhaps less exotic and appealing than many of the Eastern martial arts disciplines, but it's very realistic for training for real fighting, perhaps in combination with one of the other hitting disciplines.

Boxing is a fight sport where the only form of hitting allowed is punching. The fighters wear padded gloves and helmet. You can also train by hitting a punchbag or pads. Sparring takes place in a roped-off rectangle called the "ring". While the fighting style is quite limited, boxing is excellent for cardio training and perhaps unsurpassed for teaching you to hit

▶ *Krav Maga is a mixture of wrestling, boxing and street fighting techniques and is respected throughout the martial arts community as a practical fight system.*

hard and fast. In combination with learning some holds and groundwork, it's an excellent training discipline.

Kickboxing is also a form of full-contact competition fighting in a ring, but can be very effective in self-defence situations. The variant known as Muay Thai, or Thai boxing also uses elbow, knee and shins as well as kicks and this makes it one of the most realistic of the sport disciplines for standing combat. Tae kwon do also uses kick fighting (plus hand blocking and striking) for effective self-defence.

MILITARY FIGHTING SYSTEMS
Krav Maga is a military system developed for the Israeli security forces. It takes skills from boxing, wrestling and street fighting and combines them

▲ *Military fighting skills like Krav Maga, Sanshou or Systema are a melting pot of techniques from different disciplines worldwide.*

to create a real-world fighting art. As such, it is one of the most effective disciplines that you could learn by joining a Krav Maga club close to where you live. Training can also cover psychology and situational awareness, making it ideal for the urban survivalist.

Other similar fighting systems are taught in the military around the world. Examples are the US Marine Corps Martial Arts Program, the Chinese Sanshou and the Russian discipline, Systema. But bear in mind that without the fitness training alongside, you will only last a few seconds before becoming ineffective.

Using improvised weapons

Because of the fear of attack some people habitually carry a knife or some other weapon. Although they may see it as an acceptable thing to do as they intend to use the weapon for self-defence only, the police in most countries would regard this as an illegal act, which could lead to arrest and punishment.

However, the law does accept that at times the use of force is justified if the action is reasonable in the prevention of an attack against yourself or another person. The key word is "reasonable". It would not be reasonable, for example, if having driven off an attacker you then pursued them and jammed your pen into their eye. On the other hand, if you performed the same act because you were being attacked and believed your life was in danger, it would probably be seen as reasonable, especially if your attacker was armed.

Within the boundaries set by the law it is perfectly possible to make use of items in your possession that are not usually thought of as weapons to defend yourself. These might include an umbrella or rolled newspaper, a bunch of keys, a belt or dog lead, the contents of a handbag – such as a comb (especially if it is made of steel or is pointed), credit cards, hairsprays and deodorants, a lighter, and pens and pencils – or the handbag itself, particularly if it is heavy.

IMPROVING YOUR STRIKES

As with all other aspects of effective self-defence it is important to practise your responses in order to develop efficient technique. If you make a "weapon" from a bundle of rolled-up newspapers taped together you can improve significantly your striking and targeting skills. Hang the bundle at about head height and practise delivering fast, hard and accurate blows at the centre line of the target.

NEWSPAPER OR MAGAZINE

1 A tightly rolled magazine or paper is surprisingly rigid and can be used to deliver powerful blows to the throat and face. The windpipe, eyes and mouth are especially vulnerable to this.

2 The magazine needs to be readily accessible, so it could be carried in the side of a bag, placed in such a way that the dominant hand (in this case the right hand) can grab it quickly.

3 Once the attacker has tried to take control of you as a victim, pull the magazine out of the bag and strike towards the attacker's neck or face.

4 Grab the hair or throat and pull the head towards the magazine as it moves up. Stab inwards, driving in with all the power of your shoulders and hips.

BUNCH OF KEYS

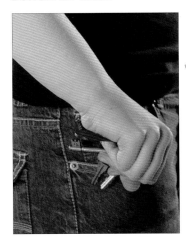

1 A bunch of keys can be used to deliver a very painful strike to the face. Keep the keys in the pocket nearest to your dominant hand, and if you feel you might be entering a dangerous place make sure that the pocket does not contain anything else that might prevent you getting to the keys quickly.

2 Pull the keys out and step backwards to create some space. This will also tend to unbalance the attacker if he has already made contact.

3 Drive the keys towards the attacker's eyes with a strong raking movement. A natural follow-up technique in this situation would be a knee to the groin.

UMBRELLAS

Umbrellas can be used in several different ways as an effective improvised weapon. A long rolled umbrella, held in either one or both hands, can be used to block someone attacking you with a weapon. Alternatively the tip can be rammed into the attacker's face with the intention of hitting the eyes, nose or teeth. Even a short umbrella, when open, can be used to distract an attacker while setting him up for a counter-attack such as a kick to the groin.

AEROSOL SPRAYS

Hair spray or deodorant can be used as an effective way to interfere with an attacker's vision. As with the rolled magazine and the keys, the aerosol needs to be carried in such a way that it can be brought into use quickly with the dominant hand. When transferring it to somewhere handy, make sure you remove its cap, if it has one, so that you don't lose the element of surprise by having to fumble with it at the crucial moment – speed and surprise are key in self-defence.

Once the attack begins, seize the initiative by stepping forwards and spraying into the attacker's eyes and mouth. Don't be afraid also to use the container as a striking weapon against the eyes, nose and mouth. The likelihood is that your attacker will recoil in pain or surprise, exposing his groin to attack from your knee or foot. Take the first opportunity to run to safety that you can.

Frontal attack

Most attacks from the front you will, by definition, see coming. That is to your advantage, giving you crucial moments to take in the situation and switch into survival mode.

Preparation for surviving a real attack must involve a physically vigorous approach. In training, the partner who is playing the part of an attacker must attempt to duplicate as closely as possible the actual situation likely to be faced to allow the defender to develop realistic responses. This is not simply about technique – a spirited attitude is very important. A man attacking a woman, for example, will generally be stronger and heavier than his intended victim. It is vital for the defender to respond with total

commitment and decisiveness and to keep on resisting, even if some pain is involved.

A study of victims of attempted rape found that those women who were used to engaging in a contact sport were better able to resist an attack and avoid being raped. This kind of habitual experience teaches that physical contact, even if it involves being hurt or knocked down, is not the worst thing that can happen, so it can be helpful in an attack.

▶ *Use a weapon of opportunity (in this case an umbrella) to continue your counter-attack. As soon as possible run away towards a well-lit area and report the attack to the police.*

TAKING CONTROL OF A FRONTAL ATTACK

1 The attacker makes his initial approach and contact by taking hold of the defender's right wrist.

2 The attacker raises his other hand as a threat. You should see this as an attempt to force your compliance by invading your personal space with a threatening gesture.

3 Break free from the attacker's grasp and slap his hand away to the side. Simultaneously, with your other hand grab his raised finger and bend it back with the aim of snapping it. If possible use a twisting action as you bend the finger back. Spitting in the assailant's eyes will also help to distract him momentarily.

4 Continue the defence by driving your knee into his groin. Meanwhile, you should scream as loudly as possible to attract attention, intimidate the attacker and add strength to your attack.

If your attacker proves stronger than you expected, don't give up. Continue to attack: bite, spit, gouge and use any chance to escape.

5 Follow through with a right elbow to the face, aiming at the nose, the throat or the temple.

6 Step backwards and pull the attacker on to your rising right knee aimed at the face, throat or other target.

7 Continue to attack with your right foot, this time by stamping as hard as possible against the attacker's knee.

8 By now he may be doubled up. Step in and deliver a dropping elbow strike to the neck or face.

9 Drive the attacker into the ground to create space to escape, or hit him with an improvised weapon such as a bag.

Attack from behind

Any kind of attack from the rear is likely to be very successful as it makes the best use of surprise and the shock of impact and minimizes the possibility of the victim using the hands and feet in defence.

A person using a cash machine is in a situation where they are vulnerable to an attack from behind, and this approach is also often used by potential rapists targeting women and girls. As an attack from the rear is based on surprise the best defence is to stay alert to the possibility of such an attack. If you have to walk on your own along a poorly lit pavement at night, walk facing the

traffic so a car cannot pull up behind you and catch you unawares. If you think someone is following you, cross the road more than once. If you are still afraid get to the nearest place where other people are – a take-away or somewhere with lights on – and call the police. Scan your surroundings continuously to minimize the possibility of an attacker approaching from a blind spot – even if it is unlikely to occur it is sensible to be aware.

Most attacks from behind will involve some grappling as the attacker is likely to wrap his arms around your upper body or grab and pull your hair.

It is important to maintain your balance and to try to destroy the attacker's balance while causing him pain. Tactics such as stamping on the foot or knee while clawing at his groin work well.

REACT INSTANTLY

Your training should prepare you to explode into your defence, going from rest to 100 per cent effort as quickly as possible, physically and mentally. Continue to exert forward pressure until the attacker is defeated or runs away.

COUNTERING A REAR ATTACK

2 Drive your elbow backwards into the attacker's ribs as hard as possible. As you make this strike you should feel as if you are trying to smash completely through the attacker's body in order to generate sufficient force.

3 With your left hand grab the opponent's left fingers, ideally the ring and little fingers. Bend the fingers backwards as far as you can, breaking them if possible.

1 The attacker attempts to grab you with a bear hug. At the moment of contact step forward as far as possible and lift your arms to minimize the attacker's advantage of strength.

▶ *If you can break the attacker's fingers you will make it virtually impossible for him to strike or grab you with his damaged hand. In addition, a relatively small slap to his broken fingers will cause intense pain.*

4 Step away from the attacker's right hand, pivoting at an angle to expose his centre line. Maintain the pressure on the fingers.

5 Push forwards using both hands to apply more leverage to the fingers; if possible apply a twisting, wrenching motion to the finger joints.

6 Reach with the right hand to grab the attacker's hair, and pull the head backwards and down while maintaining leverage on the fingers of the left hand.

7 Stamp on the back of the attacker's left knee with your right foot. Drive down with your full weight, smashing his knee joint on to the ground.

8 Once you have succeeded in getting the attacker to the ground, maintain your holds on him as you shift your body weight forwards.

9 Now push the attacker away from you and down on to the ground. Escape as quickly as possible.

KEEPING THE ADVANTAGE

As you drive forwards take any opportunity that comes by to deliver strikes to the perpetrator's body.

Head butt

A head butt can be a devastating form of attack if it lands on the nose, eye or cheekbone, and is often the favoured method of those skilled at heading a football. Its effect can be maximized by pulling the victim on to the strike, and the target area is stabilized by gripping the victim's clothing with both hands. If a head butt lands cleanly it can easily cause a knockout, concussion and damage to the soft tissues of the face. It can also lead to permanent eye damage or even brain damage.

Defending against a head butt requires fast reaction to the initial grab.

DEFENDING AGAINST A HEAD BUTT

1 The attacker has grabbed you to set you up for a head butt. Often the grab is so strong that the victim's head suffers a degree of whiplash. It is important to train the muscles of the neck to minimize the effects of being grabbed and jerked into a blow.

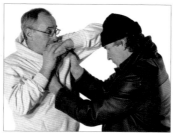

2 As the attacker drives his head forwards towards your face, lift your elbow in such a way that the point of the elbow meets the attacker's face. This will stop the head butt and cause some damage to the soft tissues of the attacker's face.

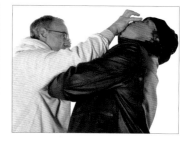

3 Drive the heel of your right hand directly into the attacker's jaw or throat, pushing the head backwards. A claw hand attack to the eyes can be delivered at the same time to further weaken and disorient the attacker.

4 Drop your body weight and jerk the attacker's arm downwards as strongly as possible with the aim of damaging the elbow joint. If space permits you should step backwards or to the side to maximize the leverage you are exerting on the arm.

5 Twist the attacker's arm up and around, forcing it up his back and wrenching his shoulder. This will force his head downwards, where it is vulnerable to strikes with the knee or foot. If the attacker manages to retain his balance, ram him into a wall.

6 Grab the attacker's open fingers with both hands and pull sideways strongly to damage the joints of the hand. You do not need a lot of strength to do major damage in this way. The attacker will then be unable to use his hand to grab or strike you.

Head attack from behind

If an attacker approaches you from behind they may not have a weapon to attack you with but want to grab you to keep you from running away. If you have long hair this makes it easier for them. It can be very painful but with a few simple procedures you can extract yourself from the attack and get away. As always, speed is of the essence.

DEFENDING AGAINST HAIR GRABBING

Step 2 detail This shows a close-up of the interlocked fingers pushing the attacker's hand onto the victim's head. You need to force the edge of your hands hard into the back of the attacker's hand at this point.

1 The attacker has grabbed your hair from behind. To avoid whiplash you have to move quickly to turn to face your attacker.

2 Trap the attacker's hand with interlocked fingers (see detail right) and push his hand against your head while turning to face your attacker.

3 Drawing your leg back sharply, continue to put pressure on the attacker's wrist by turning your head down and inwards. It is possible, at this point, that the sudden pressure on the wrist will cause the attacker to let go. If so, escape quickly.

4 If he keeps hold the pressure on his wrist will bring the attacker's head down and forward, enabling you to strike his face with your knee. Bring as much force as you can to have maximum impact and make him release his grip.

Bag snatching

A bag swinging on a long strap over the shoulder is an attractive proposition for an opportunistic thief. A safer and more discreet way to wear a bag is on a short strap under the arm, tight to the body – not that this will deter the determined mugger.

A common approach by bag snatchers is to move rapidly towards the victim from the rear, grab the bag and run away as quickly as possible. In some cases the thief will use force or the threat of force to obtain the bag. Some victims have been injured by the attacker pushing them to the ground or into a wall when the bag is grabbed. In the case of a frail victim, the consequences of the attack may far outweigh the value of the possessions that have been lost.

If an attacker makes a serious threatening gesture with a knife to intimidate you and force you to comply, let the bag go. It is not worth getting stabbed or slashed in order to keep your possessions. If possible back away while keeping your eyes on the attacker. Try to remember details of his build and appearance to report to the police later. Write down your impressions as soon as you can and get details of any witnesses.

To minimize the effect of having your bag stolen do not carry all your valuables in one place. If you

▶ *A thief intent on snatching a bag is likely to approach from behind and grab it, catching the victim unawares.*

THEFT THROUGH A CAR WINDOW

1 If you see the attacker approaching the window turn on the engine. Ideally drive away, but if that is not possible, make sure the door is locked.

2 As the attacker reaches through the open window grab his arm with both hands and pull it into the car as hard as you can.

3 Try to pull on his arm with enough force to smash his face and neck against the door frame of the car. If possible twist the arm to maximize damage.

4 Throw your weight against his elbow joint, jamming his shoulder into the front of the window. Attack his fingers and twist or break as many as possible.

have to carry a large amount of cash, put most of the larger denomination notes in an inside pocket of your jacket. Do not display large amounts of money if shopping or taking money out of a cash dispenser; this will advertise to a bag snatcher that you are worth robbing.

If you become involved in a struggle with a bag snatcher, scream at the top of your voice. A street thief depends on speed and surprise so if you can slow him down or attract the attention of others he will be neutralized.

BAG SNATCHING FROM A CAR
Even if you are sitting in it, a stationary car with an open window is an open invitation to an opportunistic thief. Whether you are parked or stuck in a traffic queue, a thief can easily reach in and grab a bag on the seat, so get wise and keep valuables out of sight.

If you spot the thief's movements in time you may be able to take action by grabbing his arm. Meanwhile, sound your horn continuously to attract attention from passers-by. Other possible responses would be to use a demister aerosol as a spray into the attacker's face, or to use a pen or pencil as a spike to gouge his arm or hand.

DEALING WITH A STREET THIEF

COUNTER-ATTACK STRATEGIES

When there is a large difference in weight between attacker and victim it is very important to react with great speed and ferocity. Like a mongoose fighting a large snake, the victim has to rely on speed and counter-attacks to the vulnerable areas of the attacker's body. Punching the stomach or chest, for example, is less effective than clawing the eyes or landing a heavy strike on the testicles or throat.

Ideally, attack the knee joints to hamper the attacker's ability to move quickly. This will remove his advantages of weight and reach, and prevent him chasing you when you escape. A stamp on the back of the ankle should damage the Achilles tendon and prevent any fast movement with that leg.

1 The attacker approaches from behind and attempts to grab the handbag, which is worn in such a way that it cannot be released quickly.

2 As soon as you are aware of the attacker's intentions, pivot to the side and deflect his arm. Pull the arm to the side a little to disturb his balance and reach up and grab either his hair or the hood of his jacket.

3 Pull his head back while stamping on the back of his knee.

4 Smash the attacker's knee on to the ground. While he is down move away as quickly as possible to a safe place.

Strangulation

Because the neck lacks any form of bony protection and contains the spinal cord, major blood vessels and the trachea (windpipe), it is extremely vulnerable to damage by being compressed. A victim will initially experience severe pain, quickly followed by unconsciousness and brain death. Pressure to the throat can affect blood flow to the brain and stop the heart beating. It takes only about 15kg/33lb of force to close the trachea; you can become unconscious in seconds. This form of attack is often directed by men against women and strangulation is frequently a feature of domestic abuse. Pressure to the windpipe which prevents breathing will quickly cause debilitating panic in the untrained victim. Arterial compression will leave to unconsciousness in a matter of seconds. For these reasons it is important to have a planned response and to implement it while you can.

DEFENDING AGAINST STRANGULATION 1

1 The attacker attempts to grab your throat with the left hand, intending to throttle you.

2 Push down on the attacker's elbow joint as hard as possible while punching him in the throat with the other fist.

3 Spitting directly into the attacker's eyes will make him blink, leaving him vulnerable to further attack.

4 Drive the left hand upwards while grabbing the hair with the right hand to pull the head back strongly. Use a jerking action to damage the neck.

5 Stamp on the back of the attacker's leg, driving the knee into the ground. Commit your full weight to the stamp to do as much damage as possible.

6 Drive his head to the ground with your palm. If he begins to get up kick his groin or stamp on the back of his ankle. Escape as quickly as possible.

DEFENDING AGAINST STRANGULATION 2

1 The attacker reaches for your throat with his right hand.

2 Parry the attacker's hand and begin to apply upward pressure to his elbow.

3 Push the arm up and over to unbalance the attacker.

DEFENDING AGAINST STRANGULATION 3

THE COUNTER-ATTACK

Do not stamp on the attacker's face or head as it could be considered unreasonable force; a stamp to the arm or hand, or to the knee or ankle, is usually acceptable.

1 The attacker approaches with his right hand reaching towards the throat.

2 The attacker seizes your throat and starts to squeeze.

3 ◄ Pull your head a little to the side, drop your chin and then push forwards, simultaneously attacking with a punch, slap or grab to the groin, intended to force the attacker to back away.

4 ► Pivot to the outside, sliding your left forearm across the attacker's throat and pulling him off balance. Step backwards as quickly as possible while pulling the attacker to the ground. As soon as he is down you can use a stamp to prevent any further attack.

ATTEMPTED STRANGULATION FROM BEHIND

1 The attacker approaches from behind, giving him the advantage of surprise.

2 The attacker wraps his right arm around your throat and begins to apply pressure.

3 Lean forwards and pull the attacker's right arm down as hard as possible to reduce the pressure on the throat.

4 Maintaining control of the arm, pivot in a clockwise motion away from the attacker, wrenching his arm as hard as possible outwards.

5 Step in with your heel behind his nearer leg while delivering a strike to his face with your right hand. A strike with the heel of the hand to the jaw or throat is very effective, especially if it is accompanied with a clawing action directed at the attacker's eyes.

6 Push the attacker backwards over your leg to throw him off balance and drive him to the ground. Once he is down continue to counter-attack with a stamp to the body or groin. Don't assume that because the attacker is on the ground they have ceased to be a threat. Move away quickly so the perpetrator cannot reach out and grab your legs and pull you to the ground.

Sexual assaults

Although anyone can be a target for a rapist – female and male – many victims are young or frailer, and most rapists use physical force to intimidate and subdue their victims. Although there is a belief that rapes are mostly unplanned attacks committed by strangers, the great majority of rapists are known to their victims and the assault itself is a result of a plan worked out well in advance.

A group attack is possibly the most dangerous situation you could encounter. The most important thing is to maintain as much distance as possible. Ideally, run away as fast as you can to a well-lit, populated area.

RAPE STRATEGIES

A potential rapist will often use one of the following approaches:
• **Gaining the victim's confidence** Usually the rapist openly approaches the victim and asks for help in some way. Once within range he becomes more aggressive and threatening. An attacker using this approach may pretend to be a police officer, a stranger asking for directions or a driver giving a lift to a hitch-hiker.
• **Sudden attack** The rapist hides in some kind of cover and suddenly attacks without warning.
• **Stealth attack** The rapist breaks into where the victim is sleeping.

Rapists try to control their victims through physical intimidation, verbal threats, the display of a weapon (usually a knife) and physical force. Often the victim is so frightened or shocked that little force is required to make them compliant. The rapist depends on this, so disrupt his plan by shouting and resisting his attack to attract attention.

Heavy drinking can make victims very vulnerable to attack. Their physical skills are impaired to such a point that it may be impossible to make use of either fight or flight, and the memory is so disrupted that it may be difficult to remember details that could help convict the attacker.

SEXUAL HARASSMENT

Sexual harassment is a threat to your peace of mind and self-esteem and laws exist to protect you. If someone calls you insulting sexual names, talks about you in a sexual way that makes you feel uncomfortable, sends emails with explicit sexual content or spreads sexual rumours about you, that's sexual harassment. It can happen in person, over the phone, or online. If you are sexually harassed at work, you may feel intimidated or anxious about going to work. Make it very clear from the outset, ideally in front of witnesses, that you will not accept any form of harassment.

If this does not work keep a record of all the incidents and report them to your employer, or ask the police. By law your employer have to take action against the offender. If, as a last resort, the continued behaviour necessitates physical action on your part, you may need to prove that your action was justified as the result of an unresolved situation.

FRONTAL ATTACK

1 Reach up and seize the attacker's clothing, or if he has long hair or earrings, pull on them forcefully.

2 As the attacker's head is moving down, drive your knee in an upward motion into his groin.

3 As the attacker falls forwards push his head backwards. Continue to counter-attack with a clawing action at the eyes.

SEXUAL ATTACK ON THE GROUND

1 When walking along a quiet lane, an attacker approaches from behind and quickly moves in to grab you.

2 He uses his weight and strength to push you to the ground, straddling you and pushing on your shoulders or arms.

3 The attacker does not have control of your legs. Hook your foot around one of his ankles.

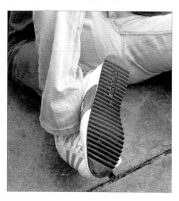

4 The ankle hook, seen here in close-up, gives the purchase you need to roll to the side, pushing hard with the arms and driving your leg against the ankle.

5 Once you have managed to dislodge the attacker, use your arms if possible to throw him into a wall to maximize the effect of the escape.

6 Drive your knee into the attacker's groin, then break free and run to a populated area. Contact the police as quickly as possible.

FENDING OFF A GROUP OF ATTACKERS

1 If confronted by a threatening group, shout as loudly as possible to attract attention and to show clearly that you will not simply accept the situation.

2 If the group persists and advances towards you, a belt with a heavy buckle, or a dog lead or chain, makes a useful weapon of opportunity.

3 A belt can be swung in fast arcs to keep attackers as far away as possible. Keep it in motion as they advance, while backing away as fast as you can.

ATTACK AGAINST A WALL

1 The attacker is hiding on a corner watching you as you approach.

2 He moves towards you quickly, pushing you back against a wall.

3 Respond instantly by driving a knee into his groin, stomach or thigh.

4 Move your head to one side and with all your weight and strength pull the attacker's face into the wall.

5 Push the attacker away from you on to his back. As he falls shout at the top of your voice and keep watching him.

6 Stamp on his groin and then run away as quickly as possible and move into a crowded area.

IF GRABBED BY THE SHOULDERS

◄ If the attacker approaches you and grabs you by your shoulders, respond by grabbing one or more of the attacker's fingers with your dominant hand. Twist and pull the finger back as hard as you can, causing the attacker's head to drop and at the same time prepare a counter-attack with your other hand. Keeping hold of the arm with the damaged finger, slam the heel of your hand upwards into the attacker's chin, forcing his head back. This will create enough space for you to move away.

Practising this and other self-defence strategies with a partner in the gym will make these moves more familiar, and will help you to respond with confidence and speed if you need to.

Attacks with knives and other weapons

While a fist or foot can inflict lethal injuries, there is no doubt that the chance of being badly hurt or killed is greatly increased when an attacker makes use of a weapon. Many objects can be used as weapons but experience has shown that the most commonly carried weapon is a knife. Unfortunately knives are relatively easy to get hold of, they are present in every home and are easy to carry and hide. In addition, there is no real skill required to be able to use one effectively.

The number of attacks using knives has risen over the past few years, and many authorities believe that a knife culture is growing at a worrying pace, particularly among young men and boys that have become caught up in gang rivalry. The claim is often made that they carry knives for self-defence, but it is also clear that blades can be and are used to attack anyone perceived as a danger or – more prevalent – as a target for theft or racial violence.

▼ *Krav Maga training with a plastic practice knife. A small amount of time spent rehearsing the defence against common knife attacks will pay dividends if you ever have to face one.*

DEFENCE AGAINST AN EDGED WEAPON

Knives or broken bottles, glasses and ashtrays can cause horrific wounds. Certain arteries are more vulnerable to attack than others, because they are nearer the surface of the skin, or are not protected by clothing or equipment. It is important to protect these areas from attack – the neck, with its jugular vein and the carotid artery, is one such area.

The most frightening thing about a knife attack is knowing that you might be cut, stabbed or even killed. Such fear is potentially paralysing. In order to regain any degree of control over the situation, you need to accept that you might get hurt.

Trying to disarm a determined attacker is very difficult. But showing that you are not one to freeze with fear is enough to put some attackers sufficiently off-guard to enable you to escape. If you are forced to defend yourself, keep it simple – and whatever you do, don't rush a person with a knife. The most likely place you will be cut is across the face or abdomen. Keep circling your attacker and at a safe enough distance to avoid being slashed

▲ *A selection of combat knives designed to cause maximum injury. Always remember that a knife with a 7.5cm/3in blade is long enough to penetrate the heart. It is illegal in most countries to carry a knife as a weapon for self-defence so don't be tempted to do so, and it can always be turned against you.*

– keep sucking your stomach in. If you can, find something to use as a defensive weapon such as a chair. Grab a coat or belt to use as a striking, entangling device, or throw any loose change from your pocket directly at the attacker's eyes as hard as you can.

USING A KNIFE IN SELF-DEFENCE

Extreme circumstances might arise in which you are forced to wield an attacker's knife to save yourself or another victim in an attack. The stomach is the best target if it is unprotected. The psychological effect of receiving even a slight wound in the stomach is such that it is likely to throw an attacker into confusion. If at this point the attacker starts to back away from the fight you should stop as well. If you are defending yourself and the attacker runs away then continuing the attack means you are now the aggressor

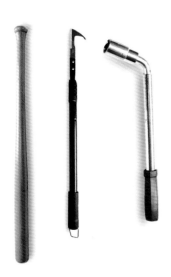

▲ *A baseball bat or other club is a common choice for a criminal wishing to inflict actual injury rather than simply threaten someone into submission. A garden weeding tool or heavy wheel brace can make devastating weapons. Always be on the alert to an attack. Anyone carrying any of these instruments walking down the street is more than likely to be looking to cause trouble.*

and you are no longer acting in self-defence.

If you are attacked in your own home, say by a burglar armed with a baseball bat, don't be tempted to pick up a kitchen knife and use it to threaten the attacker. You are just inviting the burglar to take it from you and to use it against you.

BELT DEFENCE
The belt you are wearing can quickly be deployed as a defensive weapon for whirling, parrying, tangling and whipping. You need to have the time to quickly take it off your clothing, but held by the opposite end from the buckle, it's intimidating as long as it's moving fast. It has the advantage of

▶ *A studded or wire belt is intimidating if swung or flicked at the face, and can tangle weapons to stop an attack.*

putting distance between you and your attacker. Aim to disorientate your aggressor by quickly spinning the belt around their head and face. This will keep them and their knife a safe distance from you and while they are distracted by the spinning belt you can kick out with your legs to try to demobilize them.

A metal-studded construction like the one shown below is much less likely to be cut with a bladed weapon than a simple fabric or leather belt.

BLUNT WEAPONS
Weapons such as sticks, coshes, iron bars, hammers and similar objects can cause terrible injuries. A hammer smashed down on an arm can easily break it while the same blow to the head can fracture the skull. Keep light on your feet and try to sway, duck and dodge out of the way. If you are knocked to the ground, keep rolling away from your attacker, shielding your skull with both hands and your ears with your wrists.

EVERYDAY CARRY DEFENCE
It's always good to have items about your person that can be brought into play as a defence against a weapon attack. The belt or umbrella are not out of place anywhere, but a walking stick can be deployed equally well. The

▲ *An umbrella, or walking stick, crutch or hiking pole, can be used to defend yourself against weapons blunt or sharp. Parry the attack to the side.*

wheel brace in your car is useful if you need to break the windows on your car, but it can also be utilized for self-defence. A bag or a scarf can be used to block or tangle a weapon. Everything has more than one purpose. Remember to stay within the law and only use reasonable force to defend yourself.

BEING ATTACKED WITH A KNIFE

1 If your attacker is armed the best defence is, of course, to run away as quickly as you can, but in some circumstances this may be impossible.

2 As the attacker slashes, sway back out of range, keeping your arms close to your body. Do not flap your arms wildly as they may be cut.

3 As the attacker slashes towards your face lift both arms to protect your face and neck. Do not expose the vulnerable inner wrists to the blade.

4 As you lift the arms to shield your face, don't raise them passively but smash them into the attacker's arm to cause injury or possibly loosen his grip on the knife.

5 When the slash has missed its target, grab the attacking arm strongly to put the weapon under control and drive your elbow into the attacker's ribs or face. Once you have established control over the knife arm do not give it up under any circumstances.

6 Push the attacker's elbow straight up and push your weight into him to put him off balance. Turn the knife towards his ribs. Drive forward with all your weight to push the blade into his body. If he falls, back off as quickly as possible and escape.

DEFLECTING A STABBING ATTACK

1 The attacker has grabbed you with his left hand and raised the knife to stab down towards your head or neck.

2 Move inwards to intercept the stabbing arm and deflect the blade with your forearm.

3 Grab the wrist holding the knife and extend the arm while clawing at his eyes. Push him backwards off balance.

4 As you push him back, sweep his supporting leg away from under him with your foot, causing him to fall. Try not to lose control over the hand holding the knife.

5 Use both hands to control the wrist holding the knife. Twist the point of the knife towards the attacker.

6 Drop your full weight on to the handle of the knife, forcing the blade into the attacker's chest. Escape as quickly as possible.

Gun attacks

Firearms like pistols, rifles, shotguns, automatic or military weapons are legal in some places, and not in others. In certain countries and jurisdictions, private ownership of some but not other weapons may be permissible. There may be some qualification or licence required. You may be allowed to carry them wherever you go, or only bring them out at a licenced gun range, or on your own land.

Notwithstanding, while legal restrictions may reduce the likelihood that you ever have to face a firearm, there is still a chance that the bad guys don't follow the rules, and you find yourself facing one anyway.

FACING A GUN THREAT

The advice when faced by someone with a gun in a robbery is to do exactly what they tell you to do. If they say "Freeze" or "Hands up" do just that. Many prospective robbers will carry a weapon precisely to scare you and may not even know how to use the gun properly. You are peripheral to their main plan, which is almost certainly to steal rather than murder anyone. By remaining as inconspicuous as possible, you represent less of a threat, and there is, therefore, less reason for them to escalate the crime. You also cannot guarantee whether they are a good shot or not, and the last thing you want to do is panic your attacker into firing their weapon.

But what if this is nothing to do with theft and you are the intended victim? What if your attacker has been stalking you and is trying to force you into their car at gunpoint?

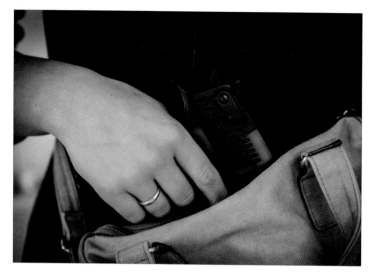

Some would argue that you should acquiesce on the basis that if you co-operate you might be able to talk the attacker round. Others say that the first few seconds of an attack offer you the greatest chance of escape and survival – by refusing to co-operate and making a scene you might just gain that crucial second to escape. Think quickly about your chances of getting under cover until out of range of the weapon.

If you do decide to run for your life, try to quickly put some distance between yourself and the attacker. Keep low and run in a zig-zag fashion to put them off their shot. If you can put some obstructions between you and the shooter, such as a line of cars, trees or a fence then so much the better, but be aware that many firearms shoot right through such obstructions.

TYPES OF GUN ATTACK
Handgun (pistol) This could be a revolver or an automatic pistol. For guidance, try to remember that revolvers usually contain six bullets and take a few seconds to reload, but automatics probably contain about ten and can potentially be reloaded very

◀ *The shotgun is a devastating weapon as well as loud and intimidating. This is an over-under double-barrelled weapon.*

▲ *A handgun could be in a bag, a concealed holster, or a car glove box. Be aware of people reaching into such things and prepare to react quickly. Lifting up the shirt ready to draw a gun with the other hand, or reaching round behind the back, are also classic tell-tale signs.*

quickly. They could contain quite a few more bullets.

Pistols are not very accurate over distances of more than about 10m/32ft, even in the hands of trained individuals, but they are extremely dangerous to be in a room with, even if the shooter is not skilled. If the gunman is close to you, you can assume he is not an expert, and try to disarm him. If he stands several metres away, your only hope is to comply or put something solid between you and him. A stone wall is good. A door, a stud-wall, or a piece of furniture will not stop the bullet. A car is worth a try, although a pistol round might pass through windows or door panels.

Shotgun Shotguns are not lethal if you are 30m/98ft or more away, but if you're close they are nasty because it's difficult for the shooter to miss. Shotguns don't shoot through much except at really close range, so hiding behind something is an option. Single barrel or double-barrel guns have one or two shots respectively and then a fairly slow reload (seconds). That can be a possible opportunity to run off to a safer distance. Auto or pump-action shot-guns can deliver eight or more rounds. Although these shotguns are limited in some countries to three rounds, your assailant may have an illegal one so don't assume you have more time than you really have.

Tasers and stun guns
A taser is a weapon that fires barbed prongs over distance trailing wires that send high-voltage electricity through the body to disable the victim. Civilian versions look like a normal handgun but with brightly coloured parts to show they are not firearms and have a range of about 5–6m/16–19ft.

A stun gun works on the same principle, but it's not a projectile weapon – the user has to press the electrodes against the person's body manually, and it can look quite innocuous, perhaps like a battery shaver. If you have an umbrella, you could open it as soon as you see the weapon. Or use it to parry the wires sideways.

If "tased" you may remain conscious, but it is likely you will not be able to control your movements. Try to avoid being hit by moving out of range or rapidly across the field of fire, or behind cover if some is available. If this isn't possible, your only option is to rush at

▲ *If faced with a taser, the most important thing is to try to avoid the barbed prongs hitting you. Try to sweep the darts and cables aside with whatever you have to hand.*

the shooter to put them off and minimise the spread of the prongs if they do hit. If hit, try to sweep the prongs sideways out of your skin as quickly as possible.

Assault rifle (AR) The weapon of choice of the mass shooter, with a magazine holding thirty rounds or more and designed specifically to kill people at short-, medium- and long-range. It goes without saying that you don't have many options if you are facing one of these. The best plan of

▲ *If that's an umbrella, opening it will provide a shield that the darts might not even penetrate and there are also more spokes of metal to catch and sweep with.*

action is to be unseen or to appear to be dead. Otherwise, in a mass shooting situation, survival will, unfortunately, depend on making yourself a more difficult target than someone else as you make your way towards an exit or something to shield you. Get low, move fast but erratically, and keep your eyes on the shooter so that you can put yourself behind objects in his line of sight.

Target or Hunting rifle Single shot or magazine? If there is a magazine under the weapon, it probably holds ten rounds or so. But generally, these weapons are used at a great distance so you won't get a chance to see it clearly. The power of these rifles is enormous, so your only chance is to hide behind something made of stone or thick metal. They are so accurate over long distances that without something solid to protect you, it makes very little difference which way you run. If you are threatened by such a weapon at

◀ *If you do take shelter behind a car, remember that the engine and wheels/brake discs will stop the bullets from most types of weapon, but the rest of the metal and glass will not. Consider that some cars have their engines at the back, and that electric vehicles don't have a large motor to hide behind.*

▲ *The crossbow is an intimidating and powerful weapon but cannot be quickly reloaded. Make that knowledge part of your escape strategy.*

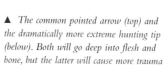

▲ *The common pointed arrow (top) and the dramatically more extreme hunting tip (below). Both will go deep into flesh and bone, but the latter will cause more trauma and blood loss.*

▲ *The hunting or target rifle, with telescopic sight and suppressor to reduce noise and muzzle flash, can kill you from so far away you wouldn't even be able to see the shooter.*

close range however, you may be able to tackle the shooter because the length and swing weight of the gun makes it hard to follow a target moving from side to side.

Bows/crossbows Archery equipment is common because it's easy to obtain, even in countries with strict firearms laws. Crossbows are aimed like a rifle and fired by pulling a trigger and are more often associated with people of ill-intent than other types of bow

(sometimes known as a longbow). This is perhaps because the crossbow requires less skill and practice to use effectively. However, either weapon can fire its arrow (or bolt) with a force that matches many firearms. This means that furniture, wood panelling and even metal offer limited protection.

The more common target tip is pointed and designed to be pulled out easily, but don't pull it out of a person except under medical supervision, because they'll bleed out. The hunting or "broadhead" tip (illegal in many places) is designed to inflict damage including, but not limited to internal bleeding. This one is effectively three pointed razor blades, which because the projectile will be spinning rapidly at

the moment of impact, will cut a spiral incision in the flesh. It's often impossible to pull out and must be pushed right through the prey.

Two things you should know about bows – that the crossbow is very slow and cumbersome to reload, unlike the longbow which can be fired again very quickly, and that if you are struck in a non-lethal way by an arrow or bolt, you should be able to keep functioning without too much loss of blood.

FACING A GUN THREAT 1

1 In a hold up like this, press your back hard against the barrel of the gun so that you know where it is and to make it harder to pull the trigger, Raise your hands obediently, but not your elbows.

2 Rotate suddenly, dropping your leading arm to strike the weapon but remember it is easier to move your body away from the gun than a strong man's arm away from your body.

3 Grab his gun hand with your other hand and strike with your knee to your attacker's groin or stamp on their shin or punch them.

FACING A GUN THREAT 2

1 When faced with someone holding a gun the best piece of advice is to obey the attacker's instructions. If it is a robbery give him what he wants.

2 If you are convinced that the attacker will shoot you whatever happens, then defend yourself. Sweep the gun to the side to get out of the way of the muzzle.

3 If the weapon goes off at this point you will be shocked by the noise, but you must hang on to either the weapon or the attacker's wrist.

4 Attack the elbow of the arm holding the gun. People are not very effective when their elbow or wrist is being bend back. Keep your body away from the gun, not vice versa.

5 Your aim is to get both hands controlling the arm holding the gun. Stamp-kick the attacker's knee as hard as you can to distract him as you make a move to get possession of the gun.

6 Pull the gun out of the attacker's hand and back away as quickly as possible. Do not be tempted to use the weapon as you could be found guilty of attempted murder.

IN THE EVENT OF AN ACTIVE SHOOTING INCIDENT

If you find yourself caught up in a mass shooting, run, hide, or fight. In that order. Run if you can, keeping out of the line of fire. Stay low and weave to make yourself the most difficult target in the room. If you can't leave the building, hide out of view or in a room, but don't leave yourself without an exit. Silence cellphones. Shelter behind solid objects away from the door and barricade it if you can. Call, text or email for help or emergency services. Do not answer the door to someone shouting for help. It could be the attacker.

If there's no escape, muster others to mount an attack together. Come at the shooter from all sides in a committed charge. With an offensive action from unexpected angles, multiple people can easily overpower a shooter in this order: gun, upper body, legs. If possible, as you charge, throw salt, pepper, or liquid at the shooter's face. Any random projectile will distract him from pulling the trigger. Grab him tightly, and hit hard to make sure the threat is neutralized.

SURVIVING ON THE MOVE

We are often at our most vulnerable when travelling from one place to another. When walking, driving or cycling we can control the pace of our progress but need to be ready to cope with the careless actions of other road users, extreme weather or the mechanical failure of a vehicle. On public transport we must be watchful for our personal safety and that of our possessions, and cope with delays and diversions. World travel brings the remote yet awful possibilities of air crashes, shipwrecks and terrorist attack. Yet the spirit of adventure defies all these risks, and with the right approach and preparation we are right to regard travel as one of the greatest of life's experiences.

Safeguarding yourself and your possessions

There's an old adage that packing for a journey is not about what to take, but what to leave behind. Most irregular travellers have a lot of luggage, and this can be an enormous burden, not just in terms of weight, but as items to keep an eye on, to worry about losing, and to attract unwanted attention.

PROTECTING VALUABLES
Dress down when travelling, and do not flaunt money or wear jewellery, other than perhaps a wedding ring. Do not carry a laptop or camera in an obvious-looking bag. Use a money belt or a more obscure hiding place on your person for carrying money and

documents while travelling. You should also carry medicines and other essentials on your person in case you lose your luggage.

If you are staying in a high-risk area it may be worth using a wire luggage protector to prevent anyone from slashing your bag in the street. Another common technique of street thieves is to cut the shoulder strap before grabbing the bag. This is very difficult to combat because the aggressor is holding a knife and is ready to use it. Make yourself look like a difficult target in everything you do, but if someone does take you on, let the bag go. It's just a bag.

▲ *Arriving in an unfamiliar city can be disorienting. For your first night, it's worth splashing out on a hotel in a central, safe location while you get your bearings.*

BAGS ON PUBLIC TRANSPORT
As well as the risk of theft, you should be wary of your luggage being tampered with for criminal purposes. Always lock your luggage or tie zips shut, and use labels that cannot be read by casual bystanders, allowing unwanted access to your identity. You might want to use a business address for added security.

Do not accept letters, parcels or gifts from strangers and do not leave your luggage unattended, even for a minute. If you see unattended luggage in an airport, train, or bus station, report it and then stay away from it.

For a small fee, many airports will shrink-wrap your bag in plastic. This not only prevents tampering but also saves wear and tear on your luggage.

FINDING SAFE ACCOMMODATION
What is safe? An expensive hotel, probably. But people come into such places to steal from the rich. Seek advice from travel agents, even if you do not plan to book with them, from people who have attempted a similar trip before, or better still from trusted locals. If you arrive somewhere by accident rather than design, ensure the provision of basic essentials like water, warmth and shade, then take time to consider what the local threats and opportunities might be before choosing somewhere to stay.

SECURING PERSONAL BELONGINGS

1 If you wear a money belt, it should not be visible in any way: keep it securely tucked under your clothing.

2 Put your trousers on over the belt, and tuck in your shirt. This way it will not be exposed by your movements.

1 In areas where luggage crime is rife, protect your baggage with a wire mesh cover like this one, which can be placed over the entire bag.

2 Close the mesh cover and secure it with a lock. You can then use the cable to fasten it either to your person or to an immovable object.

Surviving city streets

The greatest danger facing you as a road user, whether you are walking, cycling or driving, is everybody else.

As always, anticipation is the key. Keep an eye out for drivers nodding off at the wheel, reading maps while driving or using their phones. Be aware that cycles often go unseen by motorists, and that older and smaller cars often have poor levels of grip and limited braking ability. Avoid trouble by ensuring that your vehicle is in good condition and keeping your fuel topped up so that you don't have to stop where you might prefer not to. Keep a secret weapon (i.e. a rape alarm or pepper spray) in the door pocket.

ROAD RAGE

The so-called "road rage" incident is increasingly prevalent in the urban environment, where heavy traffic and hectic schedules drive the stress levels of many motorists to boiling point. The person losing their temper might simply shout abuse, but all too often the confrontation escalates into physical violence against the other driver or against their vehicle. If someone stops and angrily approaches your vehicle, lock the doors and stay inside, making placatory gestures through the windows. If they have a weapon or try to break the windows, stay calm and try to drive away if it is safe to do so. Do

▲ *Keeping safe on a busy street depends on staying alert, reacting quickly and anticipating the actions of other people.*

not under any circumstances use your car as a weapon to bump the assailant. If you are trapped, and he seems intent on breaking in and dragging you out of the car, you may have to defend yourself with de-icer spray to the eyes. A large wheel brace, kept in the driver's door pocket for accident escape reasons, is a good parrying tool if the aggressor is waving a weapon.

If the angry driver tries to ram you with his car, you are safest in your vehicle and at low speeds. So drive as slowly as possible. Don't get out, and don't try to speed off either. Even if he succeeds in making you lose control, the chances are you can wait, gather your thoughts, and drive away safely if he exits his car and approaches.

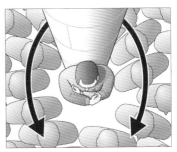

▲ *In the event of a crowd surge, say at an emergency exit, if you can find a pillar or similar structure seek refuge behind this.*

CAR JACKING

With car security systems getting more sophisticated, thieves are turning to the weakest link in the system – the driver. Car jackings at traffic lights or in filling stations are increasingly common. If the car jacker's motivation is to steal your car, the best thing to do is let them. Don't resist, and get away safely. If they are trying to force you to drive, you are probably in less danger of personal injury as they need your cooperation.

HITCHHIKERS

There is a significant risk to a driver picking up any stranger, and those who look as though they really need a lift are sadly more likely to turn out to be difficult or dangerous. Don't do it.

SURVIVING BEING HIT BY A CAR

1 When you realize a car is bound to hit you, jump just high enough to avoid the front of the car and land on the bonnet (hood).

2 Curl up on impact, drawing up your legs out of harm's way and protecting your head with your arms in case it hits the windshield or roof of the car.

3 Your secondary impact may be with the windshield, roof or road, but in each case your injuries will probably be less serious than in a direct hit.

Coping with dangerous road situations

You can run into trouble on any road journey, and of course, you cannot influence when and where things could go wrong beyond ensuring adequate preparation and maintenance of your own vehicle and keeping the fuel tank topped up. Tell someone where you are going and when you expect to arrive, and always carry a mobile or cell phone: the bane of modern life is also an invaluable lifesaver.

The number 112 is the international emergency telephone number and can be used in any country on any digital network. Due to the nature of cellular systems the success of such calls cannot be guaranteed, so you should also check for local emergency numbers. When you get through, if you are a woman travelling alone be sure to tell them so because rescue services give priority to women in this position.

MOTORWAYS

If you break down or have an accident on the motorway or freeway and have to pull over, get out on the side away from the traffic and move away from your vehicle. It is quite common for inattentive drivers to crash into a stationary vehicle in this situation.

Telephone a recovery service or the emergency services as appropriate, but stay well away from the road while you wait for them to arrive.

BLIND BENDS

If you come to rest just around a blind bend there is the danger of a collision as other road users come around the corner. Alert other drivers by placing a warning device 150m/165yd up the road from your vehicle. Stay away from the vehicle. If you have no warning device, wait 150m/165yd up the road yourself, to warn drivers to slow down.

TUNNELS

If you break down inside a tunnel it is best to get out of the vehicle but you may feel there is no safe space where you can wait for rescue. Most tunnels, however, have alcoves in the walls at regular intervals that enable you to shelter from passing traffic. Make sure you are not wearing loose clothing that could snag on a passing vehicle.

There may be emergency phones in the tunnel, but if not you may have to walk out of it to summon help. Mobile phones often work in major tunnels because aerials have been installed in

TIREDNESS KILLS

Many road accidents are caused by drivers falling asleep at the wheel on long journeys. The received wisdom is that you should not drive for more than two hours at a stretch, so leave early and build in time for breaks. Particularly vulnerable times are when you've been on the road for five or six hours (even if breaks have been taken); when you are driving when you would otherwise be asleep; and an hour after meals. Learn to recognize the symptoms (yawning, blinking and increasingly erratic driving), open a window and find a place to stop so that you can wake yourself up properly.

the tunnel for that purpose. In any case, don't linger in a long tunnel or you may be overcome by heat or fumes.

INNER CITY BACKSTREETS

If you break down in a dangerous area there may be a threat from the local inhabitants. The best way to deal with an immediate threat is to stay in your

GETTING OUT OF A SUBMERGED CAR

1 Act immediately if your car ends up in water. Get out of the car by any means possible. Turn the lights on and try to escape via a window or sunroof.

2 Wind down a side window in order to escape through it. If you have electric windows, they may well not be functioning – stay calm.

3 If you cannot open a side window by conventional means, try to smash it. Use a strong pointed object like a fire extinguisher or a wheel brace.

BREAKING DOWN ON A RAIL CROSSING

1 Don't tempt fate if your car becomes immobilized on the tracks. Assume that a train is approaching, even if you can't see or hear one.

2 Get any passengers out of the car immediately and make sure they retreat to a safe distance away from the crossing.

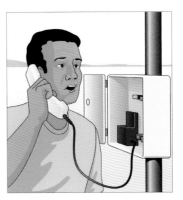

3 Use the emergency telephone by the crossing at once to inform the train operator or police that there is an obstruction on the line.

car and avoid eye contact or aggressive behaviour. If there is no immediate threat, lock the vehicle, leave all personal items out of sight, and make your way to safety, arranging for the recovery of the vehicle only when you have ensured your own personal safety.

REMOTE AREAS
If you break down in the middle of nowhere, you may be tempted to try to walk to safety. If you can positively identify somewhere you know to be within range that will afford you safety and help, then do so – otherwise, you should stay with the vehicle and attempt to attract the attention of a passing motorist. Do not risk getting lost or injured or running out of food, water and energy by setting off on a hike that has no definite goal. Your vehicle will afford you excellent protection from most dangers in a wilderness area.

ON A BEACH OR NEAR WATER
If you are planning to leave your vehicle anywhere near water you must allow for the tidal variation. Just because others have parked by the sea does not mean the rising tide will not swamp your car – locals may be parking there only temporarily. Obtain a tide table or ask for advice before leaving the car for long.

Surface conditions can also change with the incoming tide. You may park on sand that seems solid enough to drive over, but as the sea approaches or recedes, the surface may become softer or more powdery, making it impossible to drive away.

CLIFFTOPS AND SLOPES
If you park on a clifftop, or on any slope, the security of your parking brake is paramount. You don't want your car to roll away, causing accident or injury or leaving you with no means of escape. Selecting "park" in an automatic vehicle or first gear with a manual transmission is an excellent precaution. However, if you have concerns about the brake, do not rely on the gearbox alone. Place chocks on the downhill side of the wheels, or if against a kerb or similar, turn the front wheels so that the vehicle will jam against it if it moves downhill.

4 If you can't smash the window, kick it as hard as you can, starting at the corners, the weakest spots. You could also try to kick out the windshield.

5 If all else fails, try to open a door. This will only be possible when the car is nearly full of water, with the inside and outside pressure almost equal.

Dealing with mechanical failure

Breaking down in a vehicle can leave you stranded and vulnerable, but a mechanical failure while you are driving can be very scary indeed, and you need to know what action to take to minimize the risks to yourself and others on the road.

FAILING BRAKES

When you make your regular inspection under your car before driving, always check to see if the brakes are leaking. It is tempting to carry on using a car with a poor hand (parking) brake, but you should keep it in good order as it's your best line of defence if the driving brakes fail.

In the event of catastrophic brake failure you can downshift to slow the car. Many steeply inclined roads have "escape lanes" for brake failure. If you are lucky enough to be on such a road then use the escape lane. If you have to stop urgently, the hand brake will do it, but be gentle and brake only while travelling in a straight line or you will spin. Other techniques to consider are slowing down using the friction of banks of snow, hedges or ditches against the side or underside of the vehicle, but unless you have practised this before

▲ *You can plug a hole caused by a nail using rubber plug material (available from tyre repair mechanics). Reinflate the tyre or spray latex foam tyre repair gunk (available from most auto shops) through the valve, which mends and reinflates it temporarily.*

the likely outcome is that you'll lose control or the car will turn over. If you are travelling in a convoy and can communicate with another driver, it is possible to get a vehicle ahead of you to slow you down using the power of their brakes. However, this technique is only to be tried by very calm and brave drivers.

CRUISE CONTROL FAILURE OR STUCK THROTTLE

If the engine will not slow down, *do not* press the clutch or select neutral unless your life depends on it, because the

vehicle may instantly over-rev and destroy the engine. Instead, switch off the ignition immediately. The car will decelerate straight away, if anything slightly more so than normal. Brakes and steering will still work normally. If extreme circumstances dictate that you need to accelerate again, turn the ignition back on.

Some older or diesel-powered cars may not respond to being switched off – in this case the brakes are all you have, but it is still worth trying to fight the motor with these before you admit defeat and trash the engine.

STEERING FAILURE

This typically happens in one of two ways. If the steering wheel pulls off its spline, you can try to jam it back on again – it doesn't matter in what position it goes on as long as it does. If this fails, or the steering rack under the car breaks or fails, you must try to stop as quickly as possible. If you do not have anti-lock brakes you can try to lock up all the wheels by braking too hard: this will make the car understeer instead of following the errant front wheels and in an extreme case you may decide that would be a safer option.

PUNCTURE

By far the most common failure to occur while driving is a tyre puncture. If this happens you will hear a muffled flapping sound, sense vibration through the steering, and possibly feel a change of attitude (the way the vehicle sits on the road). High-speed punctures can be extremely dangerous. Put your hazard lights on, brake and stop immediately – not at the next convenient place, but right now.

If you can bring the vehicle to a stop within a few seconds of the puncture happening, you should be able to change the tyre or even repair it. If you drive on it for any distance at all you'll probably damage the wheel itself. This means that when you do stop you may not be able to remove it from the hub to fit the spare.

WHAT TO DO IF YOUR BRAKES FAIL

1 Don't switch off the engine. Shift down through the gears if you can. This will slow the vehicle down considerably, while allowing you to maintain good grip and control.

2 Once the car has slowed down to a speed of under 40kph/25mph try using the hand (parking) brake to bring it to a halt. Keep a tight grip on the steering wheel while applying the hand brake.

REINFLATING A TYRE

In extreme cases, you can reinflate a punctured tyre using lighter fuel and a match. If the tyre is still correctly seated, knock the "bead" (the stiff bit round the tyre edge that sits against the rim) off the rim on one side. For this you will need a lever such as a crowbar or very large screwdriver and a lot of strength. You could also use some sort of pipe to extend your leverage. If, on the other hand, the tyre has already peeled off the rim you need to lever it back on but make sure the bead on one side is unseated.

Squirt a small quantity (approximately half a cupful) of lighter fuel inside the tyre rim and spin the tyre to spread the fuel around inside. Ignite the fuel with a match or lighter, making sure that you keep your hands away from the rim so that your fingers don't get crushed. If it works there will be a loud explosion and the tyre will be inflated, possibly a little over-inflated. This technique can also be used to re-seat a tyre that has peeled off the rim.

Warning: This is an extremely dangerous procedure. Do this only in a life-threatening emergency.

▲ *In an extreme emergency you can reseat a tyre with lighter fuel and a lighter or match, but it is a dangerous procedure.*

JUMPSTARTING A VEHICLE

1 With the donor vehicle's engine running, connect a cable to the positive terminal of its battery. Keep the other end of the cable well away from the bodywork of the vehicle.

2 Connect the other end of this cable to the positive terminal on the vehicle you want to start. Connect the other cable to the negative terminal or another bare metal part (earth point).

3 Finally, connect the other end of the second cable to the donor car's negative terminal or an earth point. Turn on the engine, which should now start. Disconnect the cables in reverse order.

WHAT TO DO IF YOUR THROTTLE STICKS

1 If your engine will not slow down you can control the car by turning the ignition off and on as required, but do not use the clutch if you have one as this could damage the engine.

2 If there is an escape lane or a safe run-off area, use it to get off the road and out of danger to yourself and other road users, and bring the vehicle to a halt.

3 You may be able to slow the vehicle down by friction against verges, hedges, snow banks or other soft objects, but beware bouncing off them into danger or turning the vehicle over.

Getting out of a skid

The secret of skid control is to practise. You can read and hear about it all you like, but you will not be able to do it adequately unless you have tried it before. However, a few attempts on a "skid pan" to acquaint yourself with the basics are enough to give you a good chance of controlling even extreme angles of slide.

The word "skid" is used to describe any kind of slide in which the wheels are not gripping the road, of which there are many. The most common are wheelspin and brakeslides, where excessive amounts of throttle or braking respectively have caused the wheels to lose traction. These do not necessarily cause any change of direction, however, and simply easing off the pedal will solve the problem. Cornering slides, which are more challenging to control, come in three main types.

UNDERSTEER

In an understeer (sometimes called push or scrub), the front wheels do not have enough grip and the car does not turn into the corner as much as is required. It can be caused by excessive speed or braking, and it is very difficult to stop a car understeering. You can jump on the power or ease off the steering – the former adds to your already excessive speed, the latter may take you off the road or into the path of oncoming traffic.

The most common accident caused by this happens when the driver continues to turn the steering in an attempt to make the car respond, and then the front wheels suddenly grip. The car then responds to the steering and may dart to the inside of the corner or make a sudden transition to an oversteer or even a spin.

HOW TO CONTROL A FRONT SKID

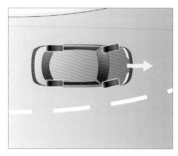

1 In an understeer, the front wheels of the car continue to plough straight ahead, so that the vehicle does not turn into the corner.

2 Reduce the amount you have turned the front wheels to regain grip and control. You will inevitably run wide of your desired path round the corner.

3 Once you have regained grip and control you can correct your course and turn the vehicle in the direction you originally intended to go.

HOW TO CONTROL A REAR SKID

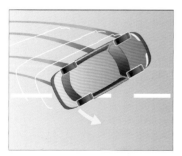

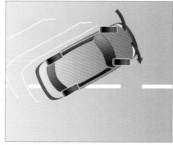

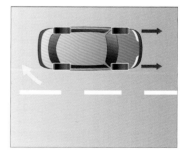

1 When the rear of the vehicle loses traction in a corner it will turn more than you intended, and could even spin right round.

2 Turn the steering in the opposite direction (opposite lock) until the front of the car is back under your control, albeit at a rather extreme angle.

3 Bring the steering back smoothly to the centre as the car approaches the right direction: keep steering the front irrespective of what the back is doing.

OVERSTEER

This kind of skid occurs when the rear wheels lose traction in a corner. The rear of the vehicle will run wide, causing the car to turn more than the driver intended. In extreme cases it may spin right around. The cause is usually excessive power application in a rear-wheel drive car, but it can also occur due to overbraking while cornering and can be caused deliberately by applying the hand (parking) brake in mid-corner (when it is known as a hand-brake turn).

If oversteer occurs accidentally the remedy is to turn the steering wheel towards the outside of the bend. Ease off whichever pedal caused the offending slide. In extreme cases you will end up with the front wheels pointing the opposite way they do in a normal cornering situation. Turning the steering wheel the opposite way from normal cornering practice is called "opposite lock".

If your car has four-wheel drive or is exceptionally well balanced you can sometimes experience all four wheels sliding in a corner ("four-wheel drift"). The same basic rules apply: ease off the throttle or brake as applicable and apply opposite lock if necessary.

Most modern cars, especially those with front-wheel drive, are designed to have a slight tendency to understeer. This is because understeer is thought to be safer for drivers who do not have

the necessary skills to control slides. Ironically, understeer is a nightmare for a skilful driver whereas oversteer is fairly controllable as long as it happens predictably.

SLIPPERY ROAD SURFACES

In ice or snow (or at very high speeds on other surfaces), the car will slide around no matter how well you drive. The trick here is to maintain a slight oversteer situation and never let the car understeer. To learn the various tricks to achieve this in different types of vehicle – front-, rear- and four-wheel drive – you may have to go on a specialist driving course. In snow, using chains or lowering your tyre pressures to about 0.7bar/10psi can really help, but you must be able to reinflate them subsequently for normal driving. On ice, narrow tyres are better, and studs or chains are best.

SWAYING TRAILERS

Trailers, caravans and horseboxes can cause all kinds of problems if you don't drive sympathetically. A trailer can cause snaking (swinging wildly from side to side) if you try to slow down too quickly, especially going downhill – the only solution is to accelerate slightly, which can be alarming to the uninitiated. At lower speeds, attempting to corner too quickly can cause the rig to jackknife and the trailer to roll over or hit the towing vehicle.

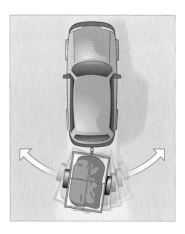

▲ *Too much weight at the back of a trailer may cause sway, which can lead to loss of control. In this case keep the steering straight – do not try to steer out of the slide.*

Even if you keep your tyres at the correct air pressure and check the treads and side walls regularly, there is always the chance of a blowout to one of your trailer's tyres. This is a highly dangerous situation, particularly if there is other traffic and you panic. Whatever you do, don't automatically slam on the brakes or try to stop suddenly. Apply the brakes gradually, and if the trailer tries to go sideways let off the brakes and accelerate a little. This will jerk the trailer back into line. Continue like this until you have slowed right down and it is safe for you to pull off the road.

ESCAPING FROM A CAR THAT IS UPSIDE DOWN

1 Push yourself up using your hands against the roof to take the weight off the seat belt buckle, otherwise you will not be able to release it.

2 If the doors won't open you may need to smash the nearest window with a heavy object. Use your arms to pull yourself through it.

3 Be aware of the danger of broken glass in the window frame, in the car and on the ground as you make your escape from the vehicle.

Fire in a vehicle

Most vehicle fires start either in the engine compartment (as a result of a fuel or oil leak), under the dashboard, or because a cigarette has fallen on to a seat. Many vehicles also catch fire when parked in tall grass and left while the engine is hot – this can ignite combustibles under the vehicle.

If you drive a motorhome or tow a caravan, you have to be doubly careful, because these vehicles contain propane tanks, which provide another source of fuel for fire. They are also prone to electrical fires because of their complex wiring harnesses. Make sure you have a smoke and/or gas detector.

USING A FIRE EXTINGUISHER
Different kinds of fire extinguishers are available, but an ABC (powder) extinguisher is the most versatile. Get a big, heavy one, to avoid the horror of the extinguisher running out, but also because it makes a very useful escape tool and weapon.

To put out a fire, sweep the extinguisher back and forth across the base of the fire until it is out. Don't spray at the flames – that won't put the fire out and will waste the contents of the extinguisher.

If you have a fire in a seat, put out the fire but then pull the seat out of the vehicle. The upholstery will probably still be smouldering: open it up to extinguish the fire, or discard the seat.

ENGINE FIRES
Fire may result from a fuel line leaking on to a hot manifold. Inspect fuel pipes frequently and replace them if they look cracked. If your engine is on fire, turn off the ignition immediately to shut down the fuel pump.

Putting out an engine fire safely takes two people, one to use the extinguisher, the other to open the bonnet (hood). It's important to get the bonnet open fast. Once the fire burns through the release cable there'll be no way to get it open. The fire will flare up as the fresh air hits it, so be ready to start spraying immediately. Don't try to put out an engine fire by spraying through the radiator or wheel arches – this won't work. You have to get at the source of the flames.

▲ *If your engine is on fire, try not to lift the bonnet (hood) more than necessary. Aim the extinguisher at the base of the fire.*

CONE OF DANGER
If you're fighting a vehicle fire, stay out of the cone-shaped danger zone, which is directly behind a vehicle with the fuel tank in the usual position at the back. If the tank explodes it sends a blast over this area that can be lethal for 15–30m/50–100ft. Some vehicles have the fuel tank at the front or side – don't assume the danger zone is the back.

Most danger is associated with petrol, not diesel fuel, which is difficult to ignite. Petrol will explode at the slightest exposure to heat, flame or sparks. So get everyone well away from a petrol-driven car.

WHAT TO DO WHEN A CAR IS ON FIRE

1 A dashboard fire can spread quickly into the engine or fuel system. Put it out at once or abandon the vehicle.

2 Prepare your fire extinguisher according to the instructions while you are standing safely outside the vehicle.

3 Reach into the car quickly and aim the extinguisher at the base of the fire. Spray until all the flames are out.

Drivers' survival strategies

If you break down in a remote area, or are stranded in severe weather, you may have to wait a long time for rescue. Your vehicle will give some protection from the elements, but in extreme cold keeping warm will be a priority.

MAKING A FIRE
Use a mirror or a car light reflector as a burning glass, or use a pair of glasses or binoculars to focus the sun's rays on to some tinder or dry leaves.

If there is no sun, use your car battery and jump leads, or any batteries and wire you have. If the batteries are small hold two together, positive to negative, and attach two pieces of wire to the positive and negative terminals at each end. Touch the free ends of wire to a bit of wire wool. It will spark up really well. If you have no wire wool touch the ends of the wires together to draw a spark. A small amount of fuel will help if your tinder isn't good.

If you have a petrol engine running and don't want to mess about, grip one of the plug leads with a gloved or well-insulated hand and pull it off the plug. Holding it near the plug or any metal part of the engine will make a big spark to light a handful of tinder. (If your insulation isn't good you'll get a very invigorating electric shock which will also warm you up.) Crucially, don't overlook the car's cigarette lighter.

▲ *In extremely cold conditions you can light a small fire under a diesel engine to keep it warm if you are stranded. Never try this with a petrol vehicle, and be very careful the fire doesn't lick at wiring or rubber hoses or seals.*

BEING SEEN
The colour of your vehicle may make it difficult to see: for instance, a white car in snow or a green one on grass. Put something brightly coloured on it such as a jumper or scarf so you will be seen and rescued.

▼ *Use blankets or coats to insulate your engine compartment to retain heat and stop the engine freezing overnight.*

LONG JOURNEY ESSENTIALS

- Car/driving documents
- Map
- Mobile or cell phone with charger, spare battery pack and emergency numbers
- Other electrical devices
- Torch (flashlight)
- Extra batteries for torch
- First-aid kit
- Spare tyre, inflated to recommended pressure, or a tyre repair kit of some kind
- Electric tyre pump
- Jack, wheel brace, locking wheel nut adapter
- Jump leads
- Tow rope
- Road flares or warning triangles
- Ice scraper and de-icer
- Container for fuel
- Basic tool kit including adjustable spanners, cutters, wire, duct tape
- Blanket or sleeping bag
- Waterproof clothing and gloves
- Extra washer fluid
- Bottled water/protein bars
- Shovel
- A sturdy plank for jacking on soft ground
- Your get-home bag including emergency food and clothing
- Fire extinguisher

DIGGING A CAR OUT OF SNOW

Dig the snow away from the vehicle's exhaust pipe before you start your engine, and dig through the snow to the middle of the underbody to allow any leaks from the exhaust system to vent. Without proper ventilation, deadly gases can quickly build up in the passenger compartment.

Clearing ice and snow from the windows and lights is a good start. Don't forget to clear snow from the bonnet and roof, or it will quickly blow on to your front and rear windows again.

If digging and spreading sand or gravel near the wheels doesn't give you enough grip to get moving, try rocking the car with quick movements forward and backwards. You can use the weight of the car to push it out of the icy depressions the tyres have settled in: be gentle with the throttle, ease forward, then rock back, until you are clear.

VEHICLE AND TYRE CHOICE

The tyres on your vehicle are its only points of contact with the ground, so unsurprisingly their type and condition are one of the biggest factors affecting performance and safety. Don't drive on worn-out tyres or try to eke out the last vestiges of legal tread depth in order to put off buying new ones. Make sure they are correctly inflated, too. Modern low-profile tyres don't tend to look flat until they are dangerously so. A visual inspection is not enough. Use an inexpensive

▲ *A vehicle after heavy snow. It's important to clear the snow off the roof, otherwise it will fall onto the windscreen. Leaving the wipers up when not using the vehicle will reduce stress on them and prevent them from freezing to the screen and getting damaged.*

pressure gauge or check at the service station each time you fill up with fuel.

Many people don't realise the benefit of all-season or winter tyres, choosing instead to drive around all year on summer tyres. Modern winter tyres function considerably better in moderate to cold conditions, even on a dry road. Anytime the temperature is 7°C or less, you would be safest using them. If it is not practical or affordable to change to summer tyres in warmer weather, it's perfectly OK to leave the winter ones on the car, although if you are making long journeys, they may wear a little quicker.

All-season tyres are not quite as good as full winter, but they are a much

better option than summer tyres if the climate where you are is temperate or colder. "Mud and snow" tyres, usually labelled M+S, are actually not as good in snow as winter or all-season tyres but they do function well in mixed slush and mud.

Be wary of placing too much reliance on four-wheel drive. While serious off-road vehicles and utility vehicles like pickup trucks have very serviceable drivetrains, many 4 x 4 road cars have systems that are designed to enhance driving stability but do very little to help in really slippery conditions. Having suitable tyres in a good state of repair makes more of a difference. However, if you're going to choose a vehicle for maximum versatility in all situations, an off-road truck with cab should be invincible on or off the tarmac. A diesel engine that can run on vegetable oil may be the best for future proofness.

◄ *Clearing snow with a shovel is extremely strenuous, so it's important to allow enough time, and to pace yourself. You won't get there any quicker by having a heart attack.*

▲ *Not all 4 x 4s are equal. This one is stuck despite having all-season tyres. Don't think because your vehicle has four-wheel drive that you are invincible in all road conditions.*

manufacture your own fuel, but it might be possible to generate your own electricity, or buy it from someone who can. An electric vehicle is worth serious consideration.

NAVIGATION

If the internet or cellphone towers are down, you won't be able to use GPS navigation on your phone unless you have already downloaded map files to use offline. Think about downloading maps now for your home region and anywhere you visit regularly. If you are planning a trip, download the offline maps for the whole journey and destination region. Considering your phone does a great job of navigating in the city, you might be surprised that when the cell signal is down, it's not good at all. This is because in a canyon, even an urban one formed of buildings, the phone can't get a GPS fix from enough satellites; so it supplements the GPS information with cell and wi-fi information.

Electric vehicles are becoming increasingly prevalent, and this might just be even more future-proof. When disaster strikes, it won't be possible to

Of course, in a state of war or electro-magnetic disaster, there may be no GPS service. Now you need maps, either paper or downloaded, and some kind of compass to find direction. An actual compass is a nice thing to have, but it's probably the worst kind. They are fragile and don't work well in built-up areas, underground, or at all inside a vehicle. They are good on a boat. But everywhere else, you might be better using the magnetometer built into your phone, and a compass app. GPS compasses exist but only work while you are moving.

▲ *A mud and snow tyre (M+S) has a chunky tread for mud or gravel and a lot of narrow slits called "sipes" which help to grip snow and ice, but on an M+S tyre they are only orientated for longitudinal grip (driving and braking).*

▲ *The winter road tyre is like a summer tyre with a softer rubber compound and hundreds of zig-zag sipes in contact with the ground at all times. This gives it unequalled grip in slippery conditions, in cornering as well as accelerating and braking.*

▲ *In conditions where all tyres struggle, the only answer is chains but these are difficult and time-consuming to put on and limit vehicle performance.*

▲ *Carry a wheel brace and jack even if you do not have a spare tyre. They are invaluable when using a repair kit or foam canister, for tightening unexpectedly loose wheel nuts, and as improvized tools for other situations.*

▲ *Make sure your GPS, cell phone, compass or watch are all shockproof and waterproof.*

Choosing a safe seat

Whenever you use public transport, whatever type of vehicle you are travelling in, your "What if?" survival attitude should equip you to choose the safest place to sit, based on experience and observation. Here are some tips to help you decide where and how to sit.

TRAINS AND BUSES

It is safer not to choose a seat at a table. In the event of a collision or a sudden stop, you could be severely injured by being thrown forward into the table, and you could also be hit by other passengers, or objects on the table, flying into you. It is safer to choose a seat where you are protected both ahead and behind by your own seat and the one in front of you. On the other hand, you need to bear in mind that on long journeys you are more at risk from discomfort – and in an extreme case from suffering deep-vein thrombosis (DVT) – than from being involved in an accident, so it may be more important to choose a comfortable seat with leg room and where you can get up and move around. If you have a choice of

forward- or rear-facing seats it is probably safer to be rear-facing, but this would depend on the nature of any accident and other factors may affect your decision.

A seat next to an emergency exit should always be your first choice. This is probably even better than being next to the main exit, since you will be in control of it, and first out of the door. Also, on aircraft and coaches such seats usually have more legroom than the

▲ *Public transport is statistically far safer than travel by car, with air travel being 27 times safer than cars in terms of fatalities.*

rest of the seating. On airlines, emergency exit row seats are allocated to passengers capable of operating the doors, which rules out the elderly and infirm and children. Although most airlines charge an extra fee to select your own seat it is worth the extra money for peace of mind.

▼ *In a train with three cars, the middle one is probably the safest since it cannot be struck directly in a collision. In a longer train, consider being nearer the rear, though not in the last two cars.*

▶ *In a single-carriage train, sitting close to an exit will mean you are first in the queue for any quick escape needed.*

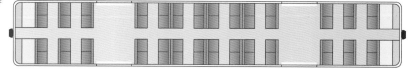

▶ *Take care when leaving a train on an open line – you could get hit by a passing train.*

▲ *Before boarding many types of public transport your belongings may be searched or X-rayed. Be ready to demonstrate that drinks are harmless and electrical equipment is what it appears to be.*

SEAT BELTS AND RESTRAINT SYSTEMS

If there are seat belts, use them whenever you are in your seat. In an accident in any form of transport a seat belt can improve your chances of survival considerably.

Do not get up from your seat as soon as a vehicle comes to a halt. This is a common cause of injury – when a vehicle stops it will actually have moved forward on its suspension, especially if it has rubber tyres. A second or so later it will rock back. If

▼ *On a bus sit on the inside aisle so that you are able to make a quick escape and also are less likely to be hurt by flying glass.*

you get up too soon, you could be thrown forward or to the floor by the unexpected movement.

As with all survival considerations, the most important thing is to think at all times about the likely outcome of an accident. Some experienced travellers, when in Third World countries, prefer to travel on the roof of a bus rather than inside. They say this is safer in low-speed accidents (which are the most common), more comfortable and healthier than being crammed in with other travellers and their livestock; in addition, it enables them to keep an eye on their luggage, which is stored on the roof and may otherwise be stolen at bus stops. This way of travelling may not be for you, but extreme circumstances sometimes require extreme measures, so you should at least be open to such options.

STORING LUGGAGE SAFELY

Most people prefer to keep their luggage close by them for security and convenience, but it is also true to say that loose luggage can be a significant danger to passengers in the event of an impact. The overhead lockers or racks are the best places for items of hand luggage that you won't need during the journey, but don't try to stow very heavy items overhead as they could become dangerous missiles in a collision. Those items you would need in an emergency should be stored about your person as far as possible.

STRANGERS ON PUBLIC TRANSPORT

Other people are the bane or joy, depending on your attitude, of travel by public transport. You'll experience the full range of human behaviour, from the travelling companion who simply talks too much when you want to sleep or be alone to threatening, drunk or abusive passengers. It's also possible that they might try to steal from you. Try to appear confident but not aggressive when dealing with fellow passengers, using firm but non-threatening body language with open hand gestures.

Women in particular may be vulnerable to unwanted attention of a sexual nature, and this attention can become uncomfortable and/or escalate into confrontation or in extreme cases sexual assault. It is safest never to travel alone – but this is not a lot of consolation if you have no choice. Try to keep within sight of other passengers or the driver, and form bonds with people you feel you can trust. Finally, keep a secret weapon handy, such as a rape alarm or pepper spray (but be certain that whatever you carry does not contravene local laws), to be used as a last resort.

▼ *In an aircraft, there is no evidence that any one part of the plane is safer in a crash, though being close to an emergency exit is clearly beneficial in terms of evacuation.*

▼ *The seats at the back are noisier and the plane moves more in turbulence.*

▼ *In a plane, the seats over the wing are the strongest and most stable but close to fuel tanks.*

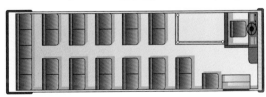

▼ *If you have to vacate a bus by a rear window be wary of passing traffic.*

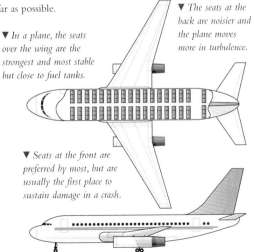

▼ *Seats at the front are preferred by most, but are usually the first place to sustain damage in a crash.*

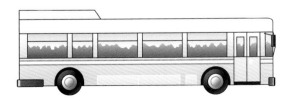

Transport accidents on land

Accidents on buses or trains generally leave you in a less extreme type of environment than those in air or water, but unfortunately they are a lot more common. Many of us are likely to be involved in one or more during our lives, in particular when travelling by road. Preparation and premeditation is key, as in all survival scenarios.

Count the number of seat rows to the exits, familiarize yourself with the operation of emergency doors, and take note of the position and instructions for any glass-breaking devices supplied. Simple things like carrying a small torch (flashlight) and a smart phone on your person, and considering your exit strategy from the moment you get on board, will always pay dividends if things go wrong.

ROAD TRAFFIC ACCIDENTS

The best protection you can have in a road accident is a seat belt. If the vehicle is fitted with them, wear one at all times, even when stationary. Once the vehicle has come to rest after an accident, release your seat belt and get yourself and others out and to safety as

▼ *Escalating congestion on the roads means that the chances of accidents and breakdowns are constantly increasing.*

quickly as possible, unless you suspect someone has a serious spinal injury. Anyone injured in this way should not be moved until medical help arrives unless their life depends on it.

If you do not have a seat belt you should adopt the brace position – placing your hands on your head with your arms against the back of the seat in front of you – if you believe an accident is imminent (see page 74). This will reduce the likelihood of injury.

ESCAPING FROM A VEHICLE

When you need to get out of a vehicle after an accident you may have to operate the doors yourself. The emergency exits may have releases on the inside, outside, or both. On some buses and trains they can simply be forced open by hand in the event of a power failure.

If you can't leave by a door you may need to break a window. Many public transport vehicles have small devices for breaking glass stowed at intervals along the passenger compartments. When you get on board, make sure you know where the nearest one is located, and read the instructions. The devices vary in type and operation and you won't be able to break the safety glass of the vehicle's windows by any other means.

▲ *Without their underground train systems, many of the world's capital cities would grind to a halt. Accidents on them are rare, but when they happen they present the rescue services with major problems in terms of access and communications.*

LEAVING A MOVING VEHICLE

If you realize you have to get out of a vehicle while it is still moving, keep to the following rules. Look in the direction of travel before you jump to make sure you aren't going to hit a lamp post or something similar. Aim to hit the ground as if running and then roll, protecting your head with your arms. If you have practised jumping off moving things such as swings, roundabouts, bicycles or skateboards you will do it better. Jumping off a vehicle travelling at more than about 50kph/30mph is probably not worth the risk of injury unless staying on board means almost certain death.

Warning: This is an extremely dangerous procedure. Do this only in a life-threatening emergency.

FIRE AND SMOKE

If there is a fire on a public transport vehicle the compartment will quickly fill with smoke from burning carpets, seat foam and plastic fixtures. Luckily, you counted the number of seat rows between you and the nearest exits, and with the aid of your torch you can crawl to an exit along the floor beneath the worst of it. Wrapping a scarf around your face will help.

ELECTRIC TRAINS AND TRAMS

Having left the train you need to negotiate the tracks. These may be electrified, so do not touch them. Look out for any conductive debris that could also give you a shock. Some electric vehicles get their current from overhead wires. Look out for these, either on top of the vehicle, or brought down by the accident.

UNDERGROUND STATIONS

If you need to escape from an underground train you will arrive on the tracks in a tunnel. If trains are still running you are in great danger. There may be alcoves at intervals in the wall, in which you can shelter from passing trains. Face outwards and keep any loose clothing or hair under control. A passing train could suck items out of the alcove and snag them.

If you don't know the direction of the nearest station, see if there is a breeze in the tunnel. The nearer station is more likely to be downwind. Once in the station, get above ground and out of danger. If there has been a fire, do not use lifts (elevators) or escalators.

▲ *Standing too near the edge of a platform carries the twin dangers of trains passing at high speeds and the possibility of falling on to the live rail.*

It is usually better to use stairs anyway as fewer people may try this way. Those who habitually use a route are unlikely to shake off the habit in an emergency.

If you are already in a lift and it stops, force the doors manually to see if you are near enough to a floor to clamber out. If not, you may be able to

escape through a hatch in the top and climb to a floor. Both actions are very dangerous, particularly if the lift starts again, so use the stop switch on the control panel before you try. Unless you are in immediate danger wait for rescue. Most lifts have a bell or phone with which to signal for help. This may not work after an electrical failure, but try it first. You can signal by shouting or banging metallic objects on the floor: this sound will carry a long way in a lift shaft.

BREAKING A SAFETY GLASS WINDOW

1 Follow the instructions to open the box containing the hammer – usually by smashing a glass cover. Use an object such as a book if possible.

2 Remove the tool and tap it firmly against the window near the corner. Make sure you break both panes if the window is double-glazed.

3 Use a bag or coat to enlarge the hole until it is big enough to use as an escape route. Remove the glass to the bottom of the pane to avoid injuries.

When things go wrong in the air

Most people fear flying more than any other common form of transport, despite being perfectly aware that it is in fact one of the safest. This is partly due to lack of familiarity – you probably fly less often than you take a car, train or bus. But another factor is the lack of control you have over your environment. In almost no other mode of transport do you have so little influence – you don't get to choose when to travel or where to sit, and you are told what to do at every stage.

You can make yourself feel much better about flying simply by being proactive about the things you can control, and in doing so you can dramatically improve your chances of survival if the unthinkable did happen.

IN-FLIGHT BRIEFING AND SAFETY CARD

If you are apprehensive about flying, the safety briefing can make matters worse by putting in your mind the idea that you are likely to experience serious turbulence, loss of cabin pressure, a crash landing and being lost at sea – all of which are very unlikely to occur. Even so, you should listen to

▼ *Members of a fire crew carry a victim away from the scene of a serious accident. The foam from their chemical extinguishing equipment can be seen all around them.*

and concentrate on the safety briefing. It is important. Read the card that explains what to do in the case of an accident. Not only will this make any emergency action less of a shock to you but you will understand what everyone else is doing, and why.

The in-flight briefing and safety card will tell you where your lifejacket is stowed. It is usually under your seat – make sure you really understand how to access it. They will also explain how in the event of loss of cabin pressure, oxygen masks will drop down from the panel above you.

The ordinary person requires supplemental oxygen at altitudes above 3,000m/10,000ft, and either aircraft must have pressurized cabins or everyone must use oxygen masks. As a result, passenger aircraft must carry emergency oxygen supplied via masks in case the cabin pressurization system fails or the plane is punctured by accident. This supply provides the necessary time for the pilot(s) to descend safely to an altitude where supplemental oxygen is no longer needed. Loss of cabin pressurization by a bullet or other puncture isn't catastrophic, as portrayed in the movies, and the loss of a door or window does not destroy the aircraft.

▲ *This plane has veered off the runway at speed and the undercarriage has collapsed on the grass, but the passengers inside may have come to no harm at all.*

FAMILIARIZATION

When you board an aircraft, familiarize yourself with everything around you. In the event of an incident it is the cabin crew's job to open emergency exits and to deploy fire extinguishers, but it can't hurt for you to make sure you know how they work. The nearest crew member might be injured in the incident, or wrestling with a passenger who is less calm than yourself.

AIR RAGE

Extreme behaviour by unruly passengers, often called air rage, can put crew members and other passengers at risk. The reasons for such aggression could include excessive alcohol consumption, a ban on smoking, claustrophobia, the tedium of a long flight, psychological feelings of loss of control and problems with authority.

Cabin crews are trained to deal with this, but in the event that you become involved, maintain eye contact and passive, open body language and attempt to calm the troublemaker. Do not escalate the conflict.

TURBULENCE AND WIND SHEARS

Sometimes the aircraft can be jerked around violently by atmospheric conditions. The pilot will usually give you some warning of this but sometimes that isn't possible so it's a good idea to be prepared for it at any time during the flight.

Make sure that anything you put in the locker above you is correctly stowed and check that the locker is shut properly after each time it is opened. Minimize the chances of something falling on you.

Don't drink too much so that you need to go to the toilet frequently or at inconvenient times. Put your seat belt on whenever you are in the seat, not just when the seat belt light is on.

PREPARING FOR THE WORST

The worst-case scenario worth considering is that you have to exit the aircraft in an emergency. The trick here is to know how many rows of seats there are between you and each of the exits. Once you have found your seat, look around and identify the emergency exits, and count the number of seat-backs between your seat and each one of the exits. This knowledge could save your life in the case of smoke, fire or power outage, since you will be one of the minority of people who will be able to find the exits blind. Anything in your possession that would be absolutely essential for your continued well-being outside the aircraft (such as medication or an inhaler) should be carried in your pockets or otherwise on your person at all times. That way you won't need to stop to grab your carry-on luggage.

In the case of smoke or fire you need to be out of the plane within 90 seconds or you won't be capable of being proactive any more. Pulling some clothing across your face as a mask can help minimize inhalation problems, especially if you can wet it first.

▶ *On water the slides may be used to get passengers out, but afterwards they will be deployed as rafts. They remain tethered to the aircraft until all people and supplies are out, or the plane is in danger of sinking.*

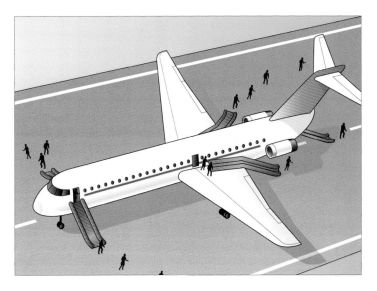

DEEP VEIN THROMBOSIS

One danger you face on a commercial airliner is deep vein thrombosis (DVT), especially if you are overweight, unfit, drink too much alcohol, or have a history of vascular problems. Blood clots form, especially in the legs, and cause pain and swelling; they may later be life-threatening if they become dislodged and block a blood vessel in the lung. Contrary to urban myth the condition is not confined to flying, and can occur whenever you sit still for many hours at a time. To avoid it, just go for a stroll up the aisle every hour, and do mild flexing exercises with your legs while seated.

Current medical thinking is that "flight socks" can reduce the risk, and these are available from airlines and travel stores. DVT is extremely rare and, while you should take precautions even if you're not in a high risk group, you shouldn't worry about it unduly.

▲ *In an emergency, escape slides are deployed from every exit and passengers are moved quickly away from the aircraft.*

Surviving an air emergency

If an emergency develops while you are on board an aircraft, make sure you have your jacket on with all essential items in your pockets. Any non-essential carry-on baggage should be left behind if you eventually have to evacuate the plane.

Ideally you should be wearing roomy, comfortable clothes that give you freedom of movement, and cover your arms and legs fully. Natural fibres give the best protection. Shoes should be low, with straps or laces to keep them on your feet in an emergency.

Fasten your seat belt and adopt the brace position. Make sure you have remembered how many rows of seats there are between you and each exit, and glance at all the passengers around you, to take in who is who and try to form an impression of how they will react if you have to get out.

EMERGENCY LANDING IN WATER
If the aircraft is forced to come down in the sea, do not inflate lifejackets or rafts until they are outside the plane. Get yourselves and all emergency equipment off the aircraft as soon as possible, remembering that fresh water is possibly the most important thing to have with you in a survival situation. Retain a line from the aircraft to the raft until everything you need is aboard

EMERGENCY IN THE AIR

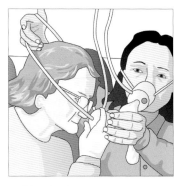

▲ *If the plane loses oxygen pressure, oxygen masks will drop down automatically. Secure your own mask so that you can breathe normally before helping others in difficulty.*

▲ *When you hear the words "Brace! Brace!" adopt the position shown here, with your hands on your head against the back of the seat in front of you.*

▲ *If fire breaks out after a crash landing, crawl beneath the smoke and fumes towards the nearest emergency exit, which you should have identified earlier.*

USING AN EMERGENCY EXIT

1 Emergency exits are opened by pulling a handle in the direction indicated. Do not attempt to operate it until the aircraft is stationary.

2 The door may open, or come right off. Make sure the way is clear before deploying a slide or other apparatus, and before attempting to make an exit.

3 Remove your shoes as they can damage slides. Jump into the centre of the slide, fold your arms across your chest and keep your feet together.

or the aircraft starts to sink – be ready to release the line and paddle away as the aircraft goes under.

If you have more than one life raft it helps to tie them together with 8–10m/ 25–30ft of line. If you can deal with it, linking swimmers together in this way is a good idea too.

If you need to search for missing people, think primarily about the wind direction and which way you, the aircraft and they might be blown by it. Any current is irrelevant because you are all in that, but wind affects different flotsam in differing ways.

Be careful about trimming and balancing your raft, but have a strategy for righting it and containing your important supplies if it should capsize for any reason.

The drier you are the better, as immersion can have adverse effects later on. If it is cold, think about ways to keep warm as soon as possible – if you deal with more pressing matters first and get cold you will probably not warm up again. If it is warm, you need to consider the consequences of sunburn or dehydration – get under cover or keep your skin covered. If you are swimming, face away from the sun or try to improvise some face covering with clothing. Obviously wear a hat and sunglasses if you have them.

Activate any rescue transmitters you may have as soon as possible. Try the radio as well if you have one. Remember that search aircraft and ships have difficulty spotting survivors, especially small rafts or swimmers. Do anything you can to increase your visibility. Keep mirrors handy, use the radio when you can, and be prepared to use the mirrors and/or marker dye if an aircraft or ship is sighted.

SURVIVING A CRASH LANDING

If fire breaks out in the aircraft after a crash landing, crawl beneath the smoke, following the floor lights if they still work and counting the seats to the exit, having identified the nearest one earlier. Go over or around anyone in your way. The chances are that some of these passengers will be lost, or just slow. That isn't your problem – don't wait in line.

If escape slides are being deployed, don't sit down to slide, just jump into the middle of the chute. Cross your arms across your chest to minimize the risk of snagging on something or injury to yourself or someone else.

Once you are out of the aircraft, stay well away from it until the engines are cooled and spilt fuel has evaporated. Check the injured and administer whatever help you can. Get out of the

wind or rain – improvise some kind of shelter as a priority. Make a fire if you need one, and make hot drinks if you can. Get communications equipment operative if possible and begin broadcasting. Having done this, relax, give yourselves a chance to get over the shock and leave any further planning and operations until later.

WAITING FOR RESCUE

After you have rested, recover all useful supplies and organize them. Remember that water is the most important thing. Determine your position as best you can and include it in any radio broadcast – if it is based on any assumptions, transmit those too.

If you bailed out of the aircraft, try to get back to it, as it will be found before you are. If it is cold you can use the aircraft for shelter while you try to build a better, warmer shelter outside. Do not cook inside the plane.

If it's hot, the plane will be too hot to use as a shelter. Instead, make a shade shelter outside using parachutes or blankets as an awning. Leave the lower edges 50cm/20in off the ground to allow the air to flow.

Conserve the power of any electrical equipment, and sweep the horizon with a signal mirror or light at regular intervals, even if you are broadcasting.

IN THE EVENT OF A CRASH LANDING

1 The pilot will attempt to make a survivable landing no matter how severe the situation: an ideal approach angle may not be achievable.

2 Whether the aircraft impacts nose or tail first there is a significant risk of the fuselage snapping, endangering the lives of the passengers.

3 The fuselage is most likely to break near the middle, and this may be accompanied almost immediately by fire in this and other areas.

Abandoning ship

Preparation is everything if you are to survive a shipwreck. Know where the lifesaving equipment is and know how to lay your hands on essential supplies: water is the most important, but also food, clothing and communications gear. If you do find yourself without a proper raft or life preserver you will need to seek out the largest floating item available, then try to transfer essential items to it.

Follow the instructions of the crew where possible. Once in the water, be rational about getting away from the ship. If it is not going to sink or explode immediately, stay with it, tethered if necessary, until all useful supplies have been recovered or it appears to be too dangerous to stay.

BURNING OIL

If fire breaks out and there is burning fuel on the surface of the water, try to make your way upwind. Burning oil is easily blown and does not spread upwind. It may be necessary to dive under narrow stretches of burning fuel, and you will need to deflate your life preserver to do this. If you have to surface among the flames, you can try to thrash your arms as you do so – this may make a break in the fire while you

get a breath, but you should regard this as a last resort as the fire will have extracted the oxygen from the affected area and the super-hot air inside a fire can burn your lungs and kill you.

You can breathe the air in a life-preserver if it was inflated by mouth. Although it is exhaled air, it still

▲ *Follow the instructions of the crew on when to abandon ship. If you are lucky, the rescue services may arrive in time.*

contains enough oxygen to breathe a couple more times. But beware of automatically inflated vests – they are usually full of carbon dioxide.

IMPROVISING FLOTATION AIDS

▲ *Knot the ankles of a pair of trousers. Swing them by the waistband over your head then pull the waistband under water to trap air in each leg.*

▲ *Cushions and pillows can be used as flotation devices. Some of those found on board ship may be specifically designed for this purpose.*

▲ *If you have no flotation aids (don't take off the trousers you are wearing), try to tread water as little as possible to conserve your energy.*

SURVIVING IN THE WATER

Don't swim if you can help it. Float on your back using as much additional buoyancy (from a life preserver, or air trapped in clothes or cushions) as you can, and save your energy. Swim only if you can be certain from experience that you are capable of swimming to relative safety. Save energy by keeping your head submerged except when you need to breathe. Even if you are a strong swimmer you may find it very difficult in the sea. Previous practice swimming in rough seas is a great help.

Swimming, even gently, reduces your survival time, and strips the heat away from your body incredibly quickly. If you stay still you will warm up a thin layer of water around you, and particularly inside your clothes. Every time you move you exchange this warm water for cooler, and lose a bit

more heat and hence energy. For this reason, keep as many clothes on as possible. If you have a bag (a bivvy bag or plastic survival bag, even a bin bag), getting inside this will trap water around you and dramatically improve your chances. Being a big orange blob is also a great deterrent to one of our greatest fears in the water – sharks (see pages 78–79).

▲ *If there is burning oil on the water, swim upwind from it.*

◀ *The best place to be if your sailing craft is capsized or swamped is close to the boat so that rescuers can find you more easily.*

EVACUATION PROCEDURES

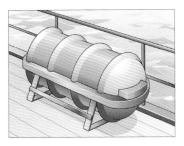

1 In addition to orthodox lifeboats, most ships have cylinder-shaped "throwover" life rafts complete with emergency survival kit.

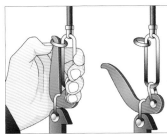

2 In order to launch the life raft, the lashings securing the two halves of the cylinder must first be released.

3 After securing the "painter" (the rope attached to the life raft) to a point on the boat, ensure all is clear below then throw the life raft overboard.

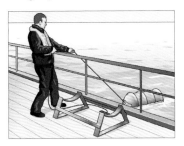

4 Pull out the entire length of the painter and then, when it is taut, give the painter a hard tug. This will start the inflation process.

5 Ideally bring the life raft alongside the boat and enter without getting wet, having first removed shoes and any sharp objects.

6 After everyone has boarded the raft, cut the painter, and look for survivors who had to jump and paddle away from the sinking vessel.

Survival at sea

When you have to survive on minimal supplies you must first look after what you have – that means firstly your life raft. Any boat will stay drier with the weight near the centre, though it will pitch and roll less with the weight distributed. In rough conditions a sea anchor off the bow can help you stay stable and facing oncoming waves, but it also slows your downwind progress. In hot climates deflate the raft a little in the morning to stop it bursting.

FOOD AND WATER
Use any supplies wisely. You can go for weeks without food, but only days without water. Drink as little as you

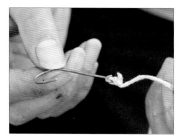

▲ *If you have some stiff wire you may be able to create a hook using any tools you have aboard. Tie the hook on to any thin string or line you can find. Try to bait the hook with something, but you may even be lucky with just a bare hook.*

can to keep yourself hydrated and if it is hot try to minimize perspiration by wetting your hair and clothes with sea water, provided this does not irritate your skin. Rain, old (bluish) ice, and the bodily fluids of sea creatures are all sources of water at sea. Do not drink salt water under any circumstances.

If you have no food, you'll have to catch some, and the primary food sources are fish, birds, and plankton. Plankton can be filtered from the sea with a cloth and are an excellent source of protein and carbohydrate if all spiny material and stinging tentacles can be removed, though you may ingest a lot of salt water with them and you should test them for toxicity.

It's easy to improvise hooks and line for small fish. Failing a line, you can try

▲ *Sharks are greatly feared, but remember that only a few shark attacks are recorded around the world each year, and not all of those are fatal. You cannot swim anywhere near as fast as a shark, but they find it hard to stop or change direction quickly – especially large ones, so you may be able to get out of the way, especially downwards as the shark can't see ahead or below once it's jaws are open. If you are attacked and have a knife, go for the eyes or gills – the most sensitive areas – or gouge with your fingers. With a bit of luck it will be scared off.*

to make a spear, but don't try to spear anything big. Birds are hard to catch but may be speared or lassoed after enticing them to land on the boat. Most seaweed is edible, while coral is always poisonous and inedible.

USING A DINGHY AS A LIFE RAFT

1 If possible attach a righting line running from gunwale to gunwale under the dinghy, which you can use to turn the boat if it capsizes.

2 Tie yourselves and your equipment into the boat if necessary, leaving your tethers long so that you will not be trapped under the boat if it capsizes.

3 You may be able to improvise a sail using a tarpaulin or even a shirt, which can move a small boat quite well and may also provide a little shade.

▲ *Sharks are careful hunters and will avoid what they see as a huge target with lots of limbs. If you group together, face outwards and stay calm, there is every chance that sharks will ignore you.*

▲ *If you can see an attacking shark, you do have a good chance of defending yourself if it's not too big. Kick with your feet or punch with a stiff arm, using the heel of your hand to ward the shark off.*

JELLYFISH

Jellyfish often have stinging tentacles, and in particular the Portuguese man-of-war and box jellyfish can cause death if the contact is prolonged and prolific. Jellyfish stings can be treated with vinegar except for a sub-group of the Portuguese man-of-war whose sting is made much worse by it, so it is safer not to use vinegar on man-of-war stings. Pluck off all the tentacles, apply vinegar if appropriate, and if possible treat with ice until the pain subsides.

To test whether something is okay to eat, hold a small piece against your skin for 15 minutes to test for a reaction. If it is alright, hold a piece under your tongue for 15 minutes to see if you get a tingling sensation. If not, eat a tiny piece, then wait for eight hours. If you have no reaction try again with a slightly larger piece and wait another eight hours. The substance should be safe to eat if you have felt no adverse effects.

SHARKS

If you're with a group of people and stranded in the sea near sharks, bunch together and face outward. Sharks are scared by strong, regular movements and loud noises so if one is close by try slapping the water with cupped hands.

If you are alone, try to float in a horizontal rather than a vertical position: this will slightly reduce the risk of attack because the shark may see you as a live target, not an easy sick or dead one. Swim rhythmically and don't panic. Sharks have highly developed senses of smell and can detect blood and waste matter from a great distance. Twilight is the most dangerous time, followed by darkness. Few attacks happen in full daylight. Shiny objects can also look like a small fish-like target to a hungry shark.

OTHER HARMFUL CREATURES

Many species of fish have sharp defensive spines that can puncture your skin, and a small number of these are venomous. Any spines should be

viewed with caution. Fish such as the stonefish and greater weaver hide on the seabed in shallow water and can be trodden on by the unwary. Other spiny fish can be accidentally hooked and sting you when you try to handle them. If in doubt, cut them loose as the venom can be fatal in some cases. If you are injured, remove the spines and flush the wound immediately. Apply very hot water and then hot compresses to try to kill the toxin with heat.

Although it is a small risk, some fish can give you a powerful electric shock if touched. If you get close to one in water, a tingling sensation may warn you of the electrical energy.

Don't take any risks at all with snakes in or near water. Some have an extremely venomous bite.

CATCHING FOOD WITH A SEA ANCHOR

1 Tie a shirt or a similar piece of cloth over the mouth of a sea anchor to act as a sieve before deploying the anchor in the normal way.

2 While the sea anchor is in use the improvized sieve will collect plankton and other small creatures as well as fragments of seaweed.

3 Sort through the marine material you have collected each day and try it out for edibility adapting the taste test described above.

Survival at the seashore

Many accidents and emergencies take place at the water's edge and it is as well to be familiar with the basic skills that can help you survive them, or to understand how your rescuers will act to help you.

There is a lot you can do to help yourself: you should be able to swim at least 50m/51.5yd in your underclothes, and to stay afloat indefinitely without wasting energy. You should also understand the basics of wave action, rip currents and tides.

▶ *The priority if you are in difficulty is to stay afloat, while alerting others to your predicament by waving and shouting.*

SWIMMER–SWIMMER RESCUE

1 A lifeguard or other strong swimmer may attempt a rescue by swimming if they are sure they won't get into the same predicament themselves.

2 The rescuer will swim to the victim as quickly as possible: this man is equipped with a towed float, which will not impede his movements.

3 The exhausted victim is carried ashore by two rescuers: the float has been tied round his waist to keep him afloat and aid the rescue.

CARRYING AN INJURED PERSON

1 Resuscitation is the priority but if rescuers suspect a spinal injury they will carry the victim ashore very carefully while supporting the neck and head.

2 The injured person is lowered to the ground as soon as the shore is reached so that resuscitation can be started in a safe environment.

3 Once breathing is restored the rescuers stabilize the victim to prevent movement and possible further injury until specialist help arrives.

LIFEGUARD RESCUE

1 A lifeguard may effect a rescue using a large, buoyant surfboard, enabling them to get to the victim quickly while maintaining good visual contact.

2 The victim can use the board as support while recovering while their state is assessed by the lifeguard, who stays on board to give stability.

3 The victim can be helped on to the board and paddled ashore by the lifeguard, which is quicker and easier than towing a swimmer.

4 If necessary the victim, who is probably exhausted, can be helped ashore by more rescuers.

5 The rescuers will check the victim over and make sure their condition is stable and not deteriorating.

6 If necessary the victim will be placed in the recovery position and checked for vital signs until medical help arrives.

RIP CURRENTS

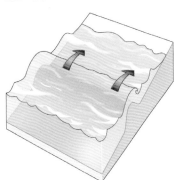

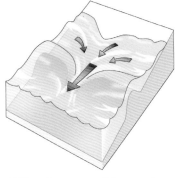

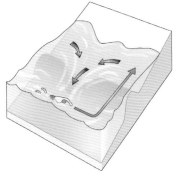

1 When waves break on the shore a significant amount of water is pushed up the beach; as this falls back it may gradually build up a sandbar.

2 When the pressure of the returning water creates a channel through the sandbar, it all flows out in one spot. This powerful outflow is called a rip.

3 A distinct flattening of the waves often indicates a rip. Swim directly across it: don't try to make for the beach until you are out of the rip.

Travelling abroad

In spite of the fact that worldwide travel is now an essential part of so many people's lives, whether for leisure or business, there is still a widespread belief that abroad is inherently dangerous, and that a citizen cannot expect the same reasonable treatment from foreign locals that could be relied upon at home. In fact the opposite is more likely to be true.

The biggest danger you face when travelling abroad is probably your own disorientation and the difference between your preconceptions about a place and what is actually happening. You need to approach any situation with the same common sense you would utilize at home, without allowing your lack of knowledge of a foreign culture to flood your mind with irrational fears.

PASSPORTS AND VISAS

You need a passport to travel to most foreign countries and a visa to remain in many. Check on the restrictions before you even begin to arrange a trip, either with the embassy of your destination country or by consulting a professional travel service. You may, for example, need a passport that has at least six months left to run in order to enter certain countries.

On arrival in a foreign country, some travellers become paranoid about their passports, carrying them everywhere as if they were a lifeline. By carrying your passport you run the risk of losing it and having to go through a lot of bureaucracy to get a replacement. In some places foreign passports are quite sought after and you would not want to make yourself a target. Hotels in many countries require you to submit your passport when checking in: instead of arguing, hand it over – it will be more secure in the hotel safe. The

▲ *As a visitor in a foreign city, you should not forget to take all the normal precautions you would at home to safeguard yourself and your possessions.*

exception to this rule is when your day's itinerary involves crossing a border – if you leave your passport behind you won't be able to complete your trip. This happens in many European ski resorts, for instance, so check before you go out for the day.

On the same note, e-tickets are much safer than paper travel documents, because you can't lose them. All you have to do is get yourself to your point of departure. Leave photocopies and details of any documents you do need to carry, such as air tickets, traveller's cheques and credit or debit cards, at home with a family member or a friend. Make additional copies for yourself and keep them separately from your documents. Consider setting up a web-based internet account and emailing such details to yourself so that you can access them from an internet café in extremis.

Make some effort to understand the monetary system in the country you are visiting, not just the currency and exchange rate with your own but the relative wealth of the local people. Carrying the equivalent of two years'

◀▲ *Legal self-defence sprays can shoot out a thick slimy goo that sticks to an attacker giving you time to react and escape. A bright difficult-to-remove UV dye helps identify the attacker days later. The rapid foaming spray (above) blocks an attacker's view and stains the face in a personal attack.*

CHOOSING SAFE TRANSPORT

The safest mode of travel depends on where you are. In parts of many cities around the world it is not safe to walk around, while in some countries driving is the most dangerous option. You'll see many people in Chinese and Indian cities riding bicycles, but it's not recommended for non-locals. In most countries air travel is advanced and safe, but there are still places you could be taking your life in your hands by getting on a plane. You should always accept expert advice and be prepared to adapt to the local conditions.

average salary around with you in case you need to buy a drink is a great way to get unwanted attention, even in fairly safe and civilized countries.

CULTURAL DIFFERENCES

It is amazing that you can get by knowing only the English language in so many places in the world. However, this is not a reason to be complacent if you are an English speaker. There are a

▼ *It's best to plan excursions in advance through reputable travel agencies or guides. Find out the duration of the excursion and how to get back to your accommodation on your return. Don't join an excursion if the transport looks dangerously overloaded.*

few language issues to consider whenever you visit a foreign country.
• Even if you stand no chance of being able to learn the language, knowing how to say "yes", "no", "please" and "thank you" goes a really long way.
• Consider whether the local language is going to be impossible to read as well as understand. If it is written in a non-Roman alphabet, you aren't even going to be able to read road signs and basic information unless you do some homework before you go.
• From the point of view of safety (or just comfort), differences in body language can be more important than the spoken word. In many ways people are the same the world over, and you

▲ *Normal modes of transport in a foreign country may be very different from what you are used to: in this Chinese industrial city many motorcycles are in fact taxis.*

will of course be able recognize something as basic as a threat or a smile. However, there can be major cultural differences and knowing about these can save you from causing offence or, at worst, from putting yourself at risk. Most good travel guides will give you the information you need on customs and cultural differences in the country you are visiting, so do your homework and find out about appropriate clothing before you go, whether any types of dress are compulsory or advisable (particularly if you are a woman) and whether certain behaviour is illegal or frowned upon.
• Knowing something about what is safe to eat is also a good idea. If the locals eat it, it's probably OK, but you may have a lower resistance to local toxins and bacteria than they do, so stick to food that has been well prepared and cooked.
• Many countries have specific local health problems that you might be vulnerable to. Malaria is a common example. While locals may not take any precautions at all, you need to check before you go whether you are at risk, and obtain the correct medication and inoculations from your doctor.

Bugging out or bugging in?

In the preparatory or "prepper" community, the concept of bugging out means escaping a situation with very little notice. Originally, preppers planned to escape into the countryside to live "off grid".

Ultimately, while bugging out might be an attractive option in the event of a localized threat that you need to get away from, it probably isn't meant to be a long term option. If the threat is indeed local, like the hurricane for example, or the flooding of your city, or encroaching forest fire, you'll be "bugging out" to somewhere relatively civilized, one would hope. Perhaps family, friends or some kind of institutionalized place of safety. You might need to walk a long way or survive overnight, but that's about as far as it goes. You aren't going to be heading deep into the forest to make a shelter, catch fish and rabbits for food, and sharpen sticks for defence. If you do need to do that, it's outside the scope of this book, but there are extreme survival manuals on the market to help you with that scenario.

In any event, if the dynamic is the breakdown of infrastructure, society or civilization itself, you are not best served by heading for the hills. In the long term, what matters is your family, your friends, and your support network. Be realistic. You can't protect yourself against looters, marauding mobs or roving bandits alone, not even with the help of your partner and your children, no matter how well equipped and trained you all may be. For this reason, we would suggest another course of action for this scenario. It could be called "bugging in".

The best place to protect yourself against the threat of other people, in the event of political unrest, a highly infectious pandemic or any circumstance that leads to societal collapse, is at home with your people around you. There's a good reason why successful people used to build castles and have people living in them rather than splitting up into tiny groups and

hiding in the woods. Guerilla tactics have their place, usually when you're on the run from something or someone, but ultimately a structure is a more practical thing to defend, especially with the help of others. If you can make your support network large enough, the optimal situation is to defend a group of buildings or entire housing development with the help and agreement of your neighbours.

Personnel can work shifts to cover security, sleep and do essential domestic chores. That's going to be impossible to achieve if it's just your nuclear family of a couple and a few kids.

THE BUG-OUT OR GET-HOME BAG

Whether you're out at work, doing the shopping, or training at the gym, you might suddenly realise you need to get home and stay home. Sometimes known as a grab bag, the bug-out bag is a pre-prepared, easy-to-carry container stocked with a selection of essentials for convenience, security and survival away from home, which you can grab if threatened by imminent disaster. If you were home already and you needed to escape the house for some reason the best place to keep your bug-out bag is by the front door. There's no time to think about what to take if the house is on fire, a hurricane is inbound, or an angry mob is advancing down the street. Just grab the bag and "bug out"! If you're out and about then the bug-out bag goes with you at all times.

There is no right or wrong with this kind of preparedness. It depends on your skills, your needs, and where you would go if you had to flee from your home or place of work, for instance. A

▶ *The Everyday Carry bag (EDC) should be large enough to carry all the essentials (see opposite) but not look out of place in your everyday life. It could equally be a handbag or briefcase. This EDC contains a water bladder, with tube and bite-valve, for hands-free drinking at any time.*

good start these days would be your wallet and smart phone. Glasses, contact lenses and essential medication are also important. Personal defence items, maybe. Beyond that, it depends on your own personal "What if?" You might need warm or waterproof clothing, or bushcraft equipment if your plan would be to go to the countryside. Food and water might be heavy to carry, but you might need to if your plan doesn't include a safe haven that provides such things. And finally, consider the nature of the bag you store it all in. It needs to be big enough, of course, but how far are you physically able to carry it? A military-style backpack might be ideal for transporting lots of small items, but is that the look you want to have walking down the road? That might attract the wrong kind of attention. A bag that goes with your location and normal appearance could be a better choice.

The exact nature of your bug-out bag is a personal decision, but below is a typical "Everyday Carry" (EDC) for your reference. It's a small bag that (hopefully) doesn't look out of place in any situation. The contents shouldn't vary much from day to day.

ESCAPE AND EVASION KIT

There are some items in your EDC that might be better kept hidden on your person than in a carry bag, in case it is stolen or taken away from you in an attempted abduction. Escape and evasion experts suggest that the best tools you could hide are a belt that can be weaponized, a handcuff key, a condom and a safety razor blade. If you're lucky, i.e. your captors are careless, these will remain on your person, whereas your bag and your smart phone will not.

Not many people realise that the vast majority of handcuffs (and particularly those used by the law enforcement agencies of the UK, Canada, US and Latin America) all use the same key, which can be inexpensively purchased online. Find a good place to hide this where a "pat down" search won't notice it. Worst case scenario is to

place it in your shoe underneath an insole, but a criminal may well confiscate shoes or boots, so try to do better.

Your razor blade is best concealed inside the waistband of a pair of trousers. It's really easy to slice the fabric with the razor and then slide it inside where it will be safe and almost undetectable. Don't forget to remove it before passing through security scanners at the airport. If you are extremely lucky your abductors will not take your belt which will make an excellent weapon. If they do take it, they won't suspect that this was your intent, so they shouldn't have heightened suspicions or awareness. Most captors will take your belt and footwear, but they probably won't take your clothes. A clever one would take everything, and search you properly, but generally people are squeamish about searching body cavities unless that's their actual job, so they probably won't do that. And that's where the condom(s) come in.

◀ *If you need vision correction, make sure you have them and spares wherever you go.*

▶ *The professional escape and evasion kit. A sturdy piece of reinforced plastic box tape, razor blades, handcuff key and condoms.*

▲ *EDC bag contents clockwise from top left: karabiner(s); notebook and pencil; sturdy gloves; multi-tool; duct tape; water filtration straw; screw-in eyelets for door bars or rope descents; stainless steel straw for drinking, self-defence and mending; mask; wireless earbuds for hands-free comms and a power-bank charger with all the cables; waterproof and shockproof phone; torch; head torch; waterproof poncho (doubles as emergency space blanket); roll of cord; spoon and fork. In the centre, trail mix food; cordless USB charger; folding pocket knife and coat-hanger wire for improvized repair and rescue.*

No one is likely to think it odd that someone is carrying condoms. If you are in a situation where you fear you might be abducted and have the opportunity, you can place important items inside condoms and hide them inside your body. They are incredibly unlikely to be found. Don't put your

▲ *This bug-out grab bag is front-loading. This makes it easier to organize your kit and find what you need.*

▲ *The bag has a full harness with padding for backpacking across the country and won't look out of place in that setting.*

▲ *The straps can be zipped away to convert it into a shoulder bag that looks in keeping with an urban environment too.*

razor blade there though, unless in a robust plastic case. Alternatives are a tampon applicator or cigar tube instead of a condom.

ADDITIONAL KIT

Clearly, this level of equipment isn't going to prepare you for every calamity that ill-fate can throw at you. A lot of preppers have multiple bags prepared for different situations. Those with a military background are accustomed to carrying heavy loads over long distances. But where does this kind of thinking end? Sure, if the threat is one that leads to the total breakdown of society or civilization, then you're going to need food, water, fuel, weapons and other equipment, and lots of it. Enough to fill a vehicle. But unless you're bugging out alone, where are you going to put your family or friends? Maybe a vehicle with a trailer

then. Are you going off-road? Maybe a 4 x 4 truck. Not going overland? Then a canoe or rowing boat.

Your bug-out bag should go everywhere with you. Because you never know when you're going to need to bug out at a moment's notice. Many of the items it carries are useful, whatever the purpose of your journey. When it comes to getting home, however, it does need to be supplemented with some other items. If you are travelling by car or another road vehicle, then clearly you can carry more gear. Much of this may relate to trying to get the car home in the event of an accident or breakdown. You may not be a trained mechanic, but a few basics go a long way. The rest of the kit should be what you'll need in order to survive if you stay with the car, and what you'll require if you're abandoning it to get home on foot.

SUITABLE CLOTHING

You will be aware of the type of clothing that's suitable for your location and climate, and you know what you'd choose to wear if you had to walk a long way. You may need warmer clothing than you are used to, to cope overnight – a thermal base layer or down outerwear is the lightest solution. If possible use the tried and tested military protocol of a full set of dry clothing and a full set that may become wet. Take off wet clothing and sleep in your dry kit. Dry your wet gear if possible. When you wake up, get back in the wet to get going unless there's no danger of getting wet again. Always keep your dry set of clothing dry, using your waterproof bags at all times.

BOATS

The ultimate bug-out transport, if you are near the sea or large rivers or lakes, might just be a boat. You are unlikely to be approached by the majority of people since they are confined to land. You can make your escape stealthily and without getting caught up in the traffic jams of road users or crowds of pedestrians. It's a good option. If you have a boat that's big enough for the

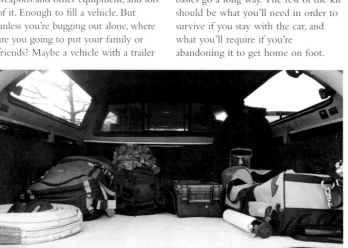

◄ *The tool bag, grab bag, camping bag and extra gear for vehicle emergencies should fit into any small car, but if you have the luxury of a larger car, flight cases are a great way to load in extra kit that can be decanted into your bag once you know what you need.*

BUG-OUT/GET-HOME GRAB BAG CONTENTS

A list of items you should consider for bugging out or getting home:
• A saw, such as a pruning saw, or a survival hand-chain saw.
• Trail mix. A pocket-size bag is suitable for a day's calories and nutrients.
• Oats. A small jar can provide breakfasts for a week. Soak a portion overnight in water. Mixing in dried milk is good too.
• Refuse sacks (aka trash bags, rubbish bags, bin bags) – carry as many of these as you can. They are invaluable for waterproofing kit, fashioning a makeshift rain jacket, or if you have enough of them, even a shelter.
• Versatile clothing. A quality down insulated jacket packs down into one of its own pockets. For less extreme cold, the fibre-pile/shell jacket can be worn against the skin and will keep you dry in all climates as long as you are active. If you need to stop, throw on the poncho from your EDC.
• Shovel. A lightweight aluminium and plastic avalanche shovel breaks down small, and you'll barely know you're carrying it.
• A couple of hats and bandanas.
• Water purification. Chlorine, iodine or proprietary water purification tablets.
• Additional water carry. The bags inside wine boxes are great as they take zero space when empty.
• First-aid kit. Include painkillers, rehydration sachets, and diarrhoea treatment.
• Wet wipes. The festival goers' friend. Toilet roll is a notorious nuisance and hard to keep dry. Wipes can keep you clean and healthy and are easy to carry.
• A webbing belt with sliding buckle adjustment. Use as a tourniquet. Or a spare belt.
• A wristwatch. If the internet is down, so is your phone.
• Two-way radios.
• A long, strong rope. Use as a tow rope, or for a steep ascent/descent or a window escape.
• A climbing harness and karabiners. You can descend a cliff or building without one, but you'll be much happier with.
• Several cam-buckle tie-down straps. Not the ratchet kind. Tie things down, tie things up, and improvise systems with your hammock, rope and harness.

The above is going to be on the limit of what one person can carry. If there are two of you, you don't have to double up on every item. Before leaving your home or vehicle, decide if you need additional equipment or if there is anything you can leave behind.

whole family to sleep and eat on and can equip it in much the same way as you would a road vehicle, it's one of the safest ways you could avoid many kinds of disaster or civil unrest.

Even if owning a substantial boat is not an option for you, it would be sensible to familiarize yourself with the operation of one, and also learn how to use a canoe or rowing boat. When a water evacuation is required these skills will make the difference between being one of those who make it, and one who doesn't. A small inexpensive inflatable boat can be an absolute lifesaver if road bridges and other communications are down. Coupled with a long length of rope, it can ferry multiple people and kitbags across a river. The boat can be deflated and rolled up into a compact portable package.

◄ *Additional really useful pieces of kit (clockwise from top left) are: a hammock and waterproof bivvy bag. It's important to get off the ground to sleep and to stay dry. 100% waterproof roll-top dry bags can organize and separate your kit while keeping everything dry. A solar panel that can recharge your equipment, either at vehicle voltage or usb. Make sure you have all the chargers and cables you need for your equipment and that you can power them from mains or your vehicle. A suitable sleeping bag that packs down really small. A spare pair of boots that can handle anything. These must be waterproof and good for a long hike. This small inflatable boat packs down as small as the sleeping bag, and can be propelled with lightweight break-down oars, hands or a shovel.*

SURVIVAL IN THE HOME

When did you last review the security of your home and its possessions? How would you guard against intruders in your house? Could you fall victim to a gas leak or carbon monoxide poisoning? Is your home a potential fire trap? If a fire did break out, would you know how to get everyone out safely? While you should know how to cope with such dangers in your home, it could also be your refuge in times of war, civil disturbance or terrorist attack. Have you considered how to make the best use of it in this context?

Guarding against break-ins

The best way to check how easy your home would be to break into is to imagine you have lost your keys and then try to find a way in, causing least damage and noise. You may be surprised at how easy it would be – and you can guarantee that a burglar will be better at it than you.

WINDOW LOCKS
For many burglaries windows are the primary point of entry, as even when locked they are often less secure than doors. Toughened glass or double

glazing acts as a deterrent, as the last thing a thief needs is the sound of breaking glass to alert the neighbours, but of course if you don't bother to shut and lock every window in the house, a burglar won't even need to consider a forced entry.

On all but the most modern factory-made double-glazed units, a window is usually secured by just one central catch. Frequently, judicious use of a garden shovel in one corner is all that is needed to distort the frame enough to allow the burglar to release the latch.

▲ *Even if you don't actually have a burglar alarm fitted, a dummy box on the front of your home can work as a deterrent.*

IMPROVING YOUR HOME SECURITY

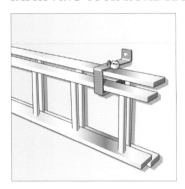

▲ *If you have to keep a ladder outside your home, secure it with a locking bracket to prevent thieves using it to gain access to your upper windows.*

▲ *Shut and lock all the upper floor windows when the house is empty, as your neighbours may not have secured their ladders even if you have.*

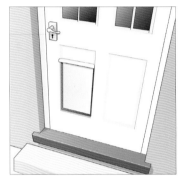

▲ *If you have a catflap in a door, you should be sure never to leave a key in the lock. An additional lock at the top of the door will improve security.*

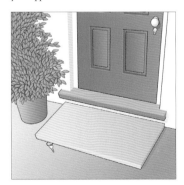

▲ *The first two places a burglar will check are under the front doormat and under a nearby plant pot, just in case you have left a spare key there.*

▲ *If intruders should manage to break into your house, you will make their job very easy if you keep all your valuables and documents together.*

▲ *If you are going away, you can make the house look occupied by using time switches in a few rooms to turn lamps and radios on and off.*

▲ *You can improvize a door bar in any situation using the screw-in eyelets from your EDC bag with a broom handle or curtain pole passed through them. It won't be as good as masonry mounted hooks but it will slow down any attacker considerably.*

To counter this, cheap and simple surface-mounted secondary locks at the corners most likely to be pried open can be fitted by anyone who can wield a screwdriver. Incidentally, your home insurance company will probably give a discount if extra window locks are fitted, but they will only pay out if you actually keep them locked.

SECURING DOORS
The front door to the property is usually the most secure, and therefore is not such an inviting entry point for the burglar. However, if the door is secured only by a single latchkey lock, it becomes a more tempting target, as this can often be "sprung" from the outside using a flexible blade or possibly even a credit card. If the door is fitted with a secondary mortise lock, or a deadlock, the thief will think twice. Not only is it much more difficult – and noisy – to force this type of lock, but should a burglar get in through a window, it precludes the option of nonchalantly walking out of the front door with your valuables at the end of the job.

Rear or side doors, often less visible from the street, are usually an easier way in than the stout front door. Always remember that a locked door is only as strong as its frame. If that's wooden, then no matter how sturdy your latch and mortise locks, their

tongues will be broken out of the wood by a firm kick or a shoulder barge. Even with multiple locks and bolts, the hinges are usually held to the frame by eight fragile screws, so it's often even easier to break that side of the door. Doors that open outwards are much harder to defeat than inward-opening ones, but they are rare, and anyway, wood is just not that difficult to break.

Door security chains or rigid door guards are usually equally flimsy because their attachment point is just screwed into woodwork or wallplugs. Implementing a secondary line of defence in the form of a "door bar", a sturdy pole threaded through two screw-hooks that are compression-bolted into the masonry, can buy you a lot of time to arm yourself and summon help.

There are many ways of retrieving a key from the inside of a lock, but if a catflap is fitted the job is easy. Larger flaps, designed for dogs, can even be used by young or skinny burglars to access the property silently, unless they are fitted through thick walls rather than thin door panels. Even if the catflap in an outer door allows access only to a porch or conservatory, breaking into it can allow the burglar to get out of sight and earshot of neighbours and passers-by, and then to work at leisure in forcing locked doors or windows into the main building.

OUTBUILDINGS AND LADDERS
Even if you secure all your ground floor doors and windows, your home is

▼ *Some sliding glass doors can be lifted off their rails from outside, but fitting a secondary lock will prevent this.*

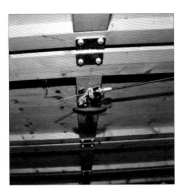

▲ *Even if the garage door is locked with a key, all the intruder has to do to gain entry is poke some coat-hanger wire in and find the cable and pull it.*

vulnerable if you leave tools in an unlocked shed or garage, and have an unsecured ladder in the garage or garden. Secure ladders on a proper rack with a substantial padlock.

Up and over garage doors, whether electric or manual, have a pull cable allowing escape from the inside, but by their nature have gaps around the door that makes it easy for someone to deploy the cable with a straightened wire coat-hanger. Once inside your garage, they can work undisturbed. Don't leave keys in your car, or any other door from the garage to the house unlocked.

DETERRING THE BURGLAR
Thieves will always go for the property of least resistance, so if a burglar alarm box is clearly visible, the side gate is padlocked to prevent anyone sneaking round the back, and there is flimsy trellis on top of the boundary wall, they will not waste time but will seek another target. They do not like gravel driveways either, as these make a silent approach very difficult. However, if you are naive enough to leave a key under the doormat or an obvious plant pot, a burglar will be in and out in a trice.

Don't make the burglar's job any easier by leaving house or car keys openly visible from outside, as it takes only seconds to snatch them through a letterbox or prised window frame with a collapsible fishing rod.

Enhancing your security

Stout locks are likely to deflect a thief's attention away from your home, but at all times you should be aware of situations that make your home more vulnerable to intruders. There are also further steps you can take to protect your property, particularly at night, when a break-in could result in an attack on you or your family.

SECURITY LIGHTING
The careful positioning of security lights on the outside of the property, activated by movement sensors, will provide a great deterrent at night. For maximum effect, lights must be positioned to illuminate the most likely entry points, and they should not be mounted in such a way that they dazzle neighbours and passers-by while allowing the intruder to work unseen behind blinding light.

If you have a garden around your home, bushes that obscure doors and vulnerable windows from view are useful to the burglar. Chop them down. (Conversely, a thorny hedge on the boundary can be a good deterrent.)

PREPARING FOR THE WORST
If, in spite of your security measures, an intruder does manage to get in at night, bolts on the inside of your bedroom door will give you a few extra seconds to telephone for help; your mobile phone should be in the bedroom with you, rather than charging up in another room, in case the intruder cuts the telephone line.

You should also consider keeping a torch by your bedside, preferably a large, multiple-battery, police-style one that can double as a defensive weapon.

VULNERABLE SITUATIONS

▲ *You are offering a sneak thief an open invitation if you leave the front door open while you return to your car to unload your shopping bags.*

▲ *An open garden door could allow your property to be burgled while your back is turned: and your insurers may refuse to settle your claim for any loss.*

▲ *Don't leave keys hanging neatly together where a burglar can help himself – especially if they include spare sets of keys for your neighbours' houses.*

▲ *Leafy shrubs growing too near your home can provide cover for a thief to hide behind while forcing an entry through a window or door.*

▲ *Window locks are only effective if you lock them and remove the key. If you leave windows open at night make sure they cannot be used to gain entry.*

▲ *Even if tools and ladders are not in full view, an experienced thief will know where to look and will use them if they are not locked up securely.*

▲ *Don't let in strangers at the door: use a spyhole or, failing that, a door chain to check the visitor's ID before you open the door.*

Levels of permissible force when dealing with intruders vary from country to country, so be aware of the law in this respect.

USING AN ALARM AT NIGHT

Finally, forewarned is forearmed. If you have a burglar alarm with a zone facility, set the downstairs circuit each evening when you go to bed. In addition to possibly scaring off the intruder, the alarm will alert you that somebody is prowling around on the ground floor and should give you time to telephone for help, get dressed, and prepare to confront an intruder who ventures upstairs.

A battery-operated stand-alone room alarm, positioned to cover the stairs, is a cheap alternative warning system if your house is not alarmed.

SECURITY CHECKLIST

Most burglaries are committed by opportunist thiefs when a house or flat is empty, more often during the evening or at night. Good security is about deflecting a thief's attention away from your house in the first place and reducing their chances of entry if they do decide to burgle you.

Around the home
• Install security lighting.
• Secure ladders, put away tools and keep garages and sheds locked.
• Don't make it easy for the intruder to slip into the garden – padlocked side gates, flimsy trellis and gravel drives are good deterrents.
• Trim back any plants or hedges near to the house that a burglar could hide behind.
• Never leave a spare key in a convenient hiding place outside – thieves know where to find them.

In the home
• Have a burglar alarm professionally installed and regularly serviced.
• Fit window locks to all downstairs windows and any others that are easy to reach. Keep them locked and their keys out of sight.
• Secure all outside doors with mortise deadlocks. Fit mortise bolts to the top and bottom of doors.
• Fit a door viewer and door chain

and use these every time someone calls. If you live in a flat, consider having a phone-entry system fitted to the main door of the building.
• Make sure that window and door frames are sufficiently strong to withstand forced entry.
• Keep your house keys safe and away from doors and windows.
• Rest easier at night by having a means of securing your bedroom door if you hear an intruder and your mobile phone and a defensive weapon to hand.

When you go away
• Keep curtains open during the day.
• Use timer switches to turn on some lights when it gets dark.
• Cancel newspapers and other deliveries when you go on holiday.
• Cut the grass before you go away.
• Ask a neighbour to keep an eye on your house – do the same for them when they go away.

If you are burgled
• If you return home and see or hear sounds of a break-in, don't go in – call the police immediately.
• If you are in the house and hear a prowler, phone the police if you can. You are allowed to use reasonable force to protect yourself or others from an intruder.

▲ *If you use a padlock to secure a gate or outbuilding, make sure that whatever the lock is attached to cannot be removed in a matter of seconds with a screwdriver.*

▲ *If a burglar does get into your home, a video camera connected to your computer can help identify him – but only if he doesn't steal the computer too.*

▲ *Keep a mobile phone, torch and other emergency aids handy in your bedroom. A bolt on the door could give you a breathing space if an intruder comes upstairs.*

Dealing with an intruder

The average burglar aims to sneak in and out of the home while the occupants are at work or on holiday, as confrontation leading to possible recognition is the last thing a thief wants. That said, if you return unexpectedly and surprise an intruder he is not likely to apologize, raise his hands, and wait quietly for the police to arrive. If you return home to find your window prised open or your front door damaged, never charge in alone or unprepared. Leave that to the police, who should be only a phone call away. You have no way of knowing if the intruder is still inside the building, or how many people are involved.

TYPES OF INTRUDER

If anything, you are more likely to encounter a sneak thief than a professional burglar. Opportunists, who are highly likely to be drug addicts looking for easy pickings to fund their habit, can be more dangerous than career burglars, as they are more desperate and therefore more likely to

REASONABLE FORCE

Should an intruder attack you in your home, you are likely to be within your rights if you pick up an item such as a child's baseball bat, umbrella or golf club to defend yourself. Likewise if the attacker is wielding a hefty blade it is probably OK to parry this with a kitchen knife, but a court is unlikely to be sympathetic if you use more force than a court decides is necessary to deter the burglar or intruder.

take chances. Should the unsuspecting householder interrupt them in the act, they are just as likely to strike out in the hope that surprise is still on their side.

Of course, there are unscrupulous types who are prepared to bully and bluster their way into a home to commit their crime, usually picking on vulnerable members of society such as the elderly or infirm. The simple precaution of checking the identity cards of callers purporting to be from public utility companies should stop this type of intruder in his or her tracks. If they do become difficult or aggressive, a panic alarm carried in your pocket or mounted by the door can be used to attract the attention of passers-by and should be enough to deter such intruders. Unlike burglars, who are mainly male, confidence tricksters can be of either gender, often hunt in pairs, and rely on their smart appearance to talk their way into your home.

While an unarmed intruder hoping not to be discovered, perhaps not even aware that anyone is home, is by far the most likely type of break-in, a more dangerous kind is the burglar or other attacker who comes armed and prepared to subdue the occupants in order to search the house more effectively or achieve some other nefarious ends. They could be armed with the very weapon used to gain

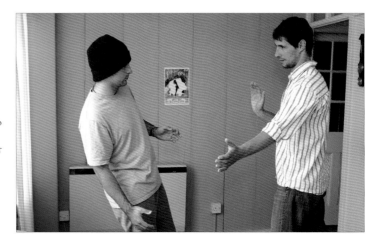

▲ *If you find an unarmed intruder in the house, don't be the one to escalate the situation. Give him the opportunity to back off, while standing your ground and showing that you are prepared to defend yourself.*

entry, like a crowbar or axe, or in the most extreme scenario, firearms or tasers. We've covered the threat of these types of weapons elsewhere.

BREAK-INS AT NIGHT

The home is the place where people feel most relaxed, and therefore it is where they are probably at their most vulnerable and least ready to deal with a confrontational situation. At night, the householder is even more vulnerable, especially if the intruder breaks or sneaks in while the occupants are asleep. Even if you are wearing nightclothes, you will still feel naked when confronted by a masked stranger, dressed in black and carrying a weapon. Should he walk into your bedroom armed with a gun or a knife, he will definitely have the upper hand. If this face-to-face meeting is in the dark, your fear will be heightened.

DECIDING HOW TO REACT

In such circumstances, many people assume that it is acceptable to use any means available to defend themselves, their family and their property, but in stable societies the law usually dictates that any force used has to be in proportion to the strength of the attack.

The official advice is to try to avoid a violent confrontation if you discover someone in your home, though in fact your basic instinct may be to lash out and drive the intruder out. If you do decide to tackle the intruder, you must be confident that you can win the fight and that you can do so without putting your own freedom in jeopardy.

It is sometimes suggested that taking up a martial art can be useful, but these specialist skills can be lethal; bear in mind that if you kill or seriously injure an intruder, you could be punished for making unreasonable use of force.

If you decide to take the submissive route, particularly if you are female, the intruder may take violent advantage of this, whereas a show of bravado and

confidence may well cause him to flee. Only you can make this split-second decision, based on your reading of the situation at the time. It is, however, worth bearing in mind that the intruder does not know for sure what lies in store, so his nerves are going to be on edge. A sudden loud noise, such as the sound of a personal alarm, could be enough to frighten him off the premises. Likewise, if he has broken in at night, a burst of bright light from a high-powered torch shone in his eyes may temporarily disorient him.

If a confrontation does develop, your positive mental attitude and confident body posture may well be enough to allow you regain control of the situation, but you should remember that if the attacker calls your bluff he is unlikely to fight clean. On the other hand, a screaming and pummelling

▲ *In self-defence, the palm strike is very effective. Cock your wrist and curl your fingers and thumb in. Aim for the jaw.*

woman with right on her side, however small and slight, can be enough to scare off a burly intruder twice her weight if he is unprepared for the onslaught. In many situations, the thief or assailant will simply try to escape if "caught on the job". Let him go. Property is replaceable, your life is not.

TACKLING A BURGLAR

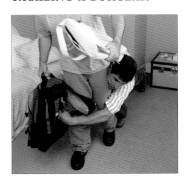

1 ◄ Remember, if you can avoid a fight do so because property is not worth risking a life for. But if you believe you or a family member are at risk then go for a lunge from behind.

2 ► A rugby-style tackle is an effective way to bring someone who is moving away from you to his knees.

4 ◄ Once on the ground you must immobilize the intruder and at the same time shout at the top of your voice for help if you haven't already done so.

5 ▼ Only confront the intruder with a weapon as a last resort.

3 ▼ Drive your shoulder into the intruder's legs while gripping around his knees and squeezing until he falls. The intruder will quite possibly be disoriented by being tackled in such a decisive way.

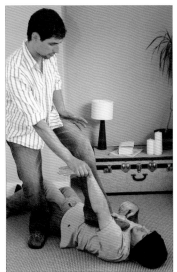

Fire in the home

Although fire is the single greatest killer in the home environment, the vast majority of home fires would be easily avoided by taking some basic precautions. The kitchen is the most dangerous room in the house and is the seat of most daytime fires, but if a member of the household is a smoker, the chances of being involved in a night-time fire increase dramatically. Unguarded candles, the least technological way of lighting a room and a favourite in romantic or party settings, also pose a high risk of fire, as do the many electrical appliances used around the home. Awareness of potential fire risks is half the prevention battle, and most of the following advice is really just common sense.

SMOKE ALARMS

If a fire does break out, a functioning smoke alarm should give the occupants a few extra vital minutes to organize an escape, call the fire service, and possibly even attempt to bring the fire under control. At night, a smoke alarm will save lives, as smoke and gases produced by a fire can silently kill sleeping occupants before they become aware that their home is ablaze.

▼ *In less than 60 seconds a small fire can fill your home with smoke. Firemen have breathing apparatus – you don't so get out fast. If any closed door feels warm when touched, do not open it - the fire is on the other side. Go to the windows instead.*

Ceiling-mounted smoke alarms are cheap and easy to fit, though they are as much use as a chocolate fireguard if their batteries are not checked regularly.

AVOIDING FIRE

Prevention is always better than cure, so when deep frying, which is the largest single cause of kitchen fires, never fill the pan more than one third full, and never ever leave it unattended.

To extinguish a pan fire, turn off the heat source and throw a fire blanket, or a damp towel, over it to extinguish the flames. Never throw water on an oil fire, as that will make the flames flare up and spray burning oil outside the pan, igniting other combustibles. A small fire blanket, suitable for tackling most accidental fires in the kitchen, is an inexpensive necessity often overlooked. If you tackle a pan fire yourself, remember that cooking fat

▲ *A domestic fire at night can be a killer, though it is usually the smoke rather than the flames that proves lethal. Go to the window and wait for the fire brigade.*

▼ *If someone's clothes catch fire, roll them on the floor and smother the flames using a blanket or rug or large coat. Keep low at all times as it's easier to breathe.*

▲ *Carbon monoxide is a silent killer – gas-fired central heating boilers and water heaters should be checked and serviced annually.*

retains its temperature for a long time, and it may well reignite if you remove the blanket too soon. Vacate the premises and summon the fire service.

The easiest precaution to take against fires caused by cigarettes is to ban smoking completely inside the house. Unlike cooking fires, which flare up quickly, most cigarette fires start gradually, sometimes hours after a smouldering end has fallen unnoticed into upholstery or bedclothes.

The precautions needed to prevent electrical fires are simple: switch off and unplug appliances when not in use, and never overload wall sockets. Even when an appliance is switched off, it may still be drawing power from a live wall socket unless physically unplugged. Televisions left on standby mode and, to a lesser extent, video recorders and digital boxes are all potential time bombs if they

◀ *Pull, Aim, Squeeze, Sweep (PASS) is a good tip to remember. Aim low, point the extinguisher at the base of the fire and sweep from side to side.*

develop an electrical fault or there is a power surge during an electrical storm. Bad wiring or overloaded sockets, usually identifiable through the plugs being overly hot, should be remedied immediately. Make sure that any cables running on the floor do not get trapped or pinched by furniture, and that any long cables drawing a lot of power are not coiled, as both circumstances can cause wires to overheat and ignite out of the blue.

ESCAPING FROM A FIRE

If fire does break out, your first priority is to get everybody out as fast as possible. Do not stop to dress properly or collect valuables. Most fire deaths are caused by inhalation of smoke and noxious gases rather than burns. Furnishings, once ignited, burn with incredible intensity and very quickly produce dense toxic fumes. To survive this you not only have to get out very quickly, but you also need to stay as close to the floor as possible, as that is where any oxygen will be.

Do not assume that the air at head height is breathable if it is free of smoke, as some by-products of building fires are virtually clear. The first you will know about them is when they burn your throat and lungs, as you try to take your last gulping breaths. Burning plastics and upholstery rapidly produce thick clouds of acrid smoke, and even at ground level you may find breathing difficult. A wet cloth over your mouth and nose will act as a temporary respirator; even a dry

▼ *Blocking any gaps by the door helps to keep fumes out of the room you are in and may deprive a fire of oxygen.*

handkerchief or shirt tail may keep out larger toxic particles. You will need to remember the layout of the room to find your exit route, as even if it is not dark you will be blinded by the smoke.

Once clear of danger outside, alert any neighbours and call the fire service. Do not go back in. Material possessions can be replaced, but your life cannot.

FIRE IN A HIGH RISE BLOCK

High rise buildings, such as apartments and blocks of flats, have been designed with fire safety as a priority. The flat's doors, walls and floors are all designed to stop fire and smoke spreading, but this relies on the doors being kept shut. If you have a fire in your flat then leave the flat immediately and shut the door. Only use designated fire escape routes to exit the building. Once out, stay out.

If there is a fire somewhere in the block of flats then the safest option is usually to remain in your flat with the doors closed. If, however, your flat becomes affected by smoke or fire then leave at once, closing windows and doors behind you. Use only designated escape routes and never the lift.

If fire is preventing you from leaving, go to the balcony, but don't think about jumping, wait for the fire brigade. Open the window and wave a sheet to let the firefighters know that you are still in the building. If you can, pack cushions, bedding or towels at the bottom of the door too your flat to block the smoke. If you have any water, wet the door if it starts to get hot.

▼ *If you have to escape from an upper floor of your house try to find ways to lower yourself to safety rather than jumping, to reduce the height of your fall.*

Gas leaks

The most common cause of damage, injury and even death in the home is undoubtedly fire. However, gas incidents, though much less common, can be equally deadly. In much of the Western world, bottled or mains gas provides the fuel for the bulk of our heating and hot water systems, as it is more efficient and more ecologically sound than coal and oil. In the past, domestic gas was derived from coal and was a smelly substance, but modern natural gas is odourless and so has to have a smell added to alert us to leaks.

Gas, like water, will always find any leaks in pipes, joints and appliances. Unlike water, it is highly explosive, so it is imperative that you are both familiar with its artificial smell, and that you attend to any leakage immediately. Do

not try to repair a gas leak yourself, as this is a highly skilled job that can be very dangerous if tackled by a novice.

If you smell gas you should immediately open windows to vent the building and get outside as quickly as possible. The main supply valve, whether you are using bottled or mains gas, is usually located outside the building, next to the meter if you are on a mains supply, and should be turned off if at all possible. If you don't know where your gas valve is, go and check now!

Once you are clear of the building, hopefully having been able to vent it and turn off the supply, contact the service provider or the emergency services. Gas leaks can cause massive damage and those responsible for

▲ *Check your vents have not got clogged up with growing plants.*

prevention would much rather be called out before the explosion, even if it is a well-intentioned false alarm, than have to pick up the pieces afterwards.

CARBON MONOXIDE POISONING

It is not only the gas supply that can be potentially dangerous in a domestic situation. The by-products of combustion can also poison the occupants if gas appliances such as heaters and stoves are not working efficiently and properly vented.

Carbon monoxide is a silent killer that works by first inducing sleep before poisoning the body. Even if the poisoning is not fatal it can cause permanent neurological damage. The gas is odourless, tasteless and colourless, so a special detector is necessary to check for its presence.

To ensure that your home is safe, all gas appliances should be checked and serviced at least once a year, particularly after having lain unused for any length of time, and flues must never be blocked or obstructed. Birds' nests, and even ivy or other creeping plants growing on outside walls, can very easily block a flue during the summer months, turning the home into a death trap when the heating system is fired up again in the autumn.

The first signs of carbon monoxide poisoning are sudden unexpected drowsiness and headache, and first aid for an unconscious victim is access to fresh air and artificial respiration.

DEALING WITH A GAS LEAK

1 Open all the windows to ventilate the building and disperse escaped gas.

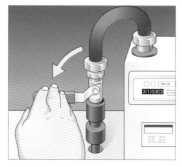

2 Turn off the mains supply by the valve near the meter.

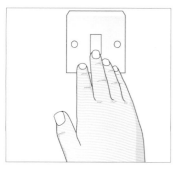

3 Do not switch on lights as this could create a spark and ignite the gas.

4 Report a leak immediately to the gas supplier or the emergency services.

Flooding

Water leaks in the home can cause untold damage. The primary causes are burst pipes during the thaw after a winter freeze, overflowing baths and faulty washing machines. Water spreads at an alarming rate and it does not take long for it to permeate into the fabric of a building. Burst mains pipes can be disastrous as the high flow rate can undermine foundations, but even an upstairs bath left overflowing for five minutes is likely to short-circuit the

▼ *If your home is prone to flooding, keep a supply of sandbags, ready-filled, with which to create barriers in front of doorways.*

electrical supply and damage the ceiling below to such an extent that a complete replacement is necessary.

NATURAL FLOODS

If you are one of those living in an area prone to natural flooding, the risks are of a totally different order. You should be alert to flood warnings and familiar with local plans for dealing with such a disaster. Simple precautions like having sandbags ready-filled and heavy duty

▼ *If you do not know where the main stopcock for your home's water supply is located, go and check it out right now.*

▲ *Freak weather can quickly cause flooding in low-lying residential areas: is your home in a vulnerable situation?*

plastic on hand to block doors may help, but if your home is subjected to a major flood, follow the advice of your local authority and emergency services.

If you have to leave your home, do not be tempted to walk through flowing flood water. Even if it does not appear to be very deep it may have a deceptively fast current that could sweep you off your feet, and there may well also be dangerous debris below the surface that could cause serious injury.

After drowning, electrocution is the second most common cause of death following a flood: stay well away from power cables and do not attempt to use electrical equipment that has been wet. You should also check for gas leaks in case the pipework has been damaged. A flood is likely to contaminate your water supply, so if you are at risk from flooding it is sensible to keep an emergency supply of bottled water.

Emergency escape

In a fire or gas emergency, it is imperative that you get yourself and any other occupants out of the building as quickly as possible. In a domestic situation you should be well aware of your primary escape route, but if fire is barring your way, you will need to seek an alternative. Despite what you may have seen in television dramas and on the cinema screen, the staircase is usually of sufficiently robust construction to survive the early stages of a house fire, and in most multiple occupancy buildings it will be reinforced and protected to afford a safe escape route. In some circumstances, however, especially if fire doors have been left open, use of the staircase may not be possible and you may need to use a window instead.

ESCAPING THROUGH A WINDOW

If window locks are fitted, the key should be kept in a place where it is easy to find, especially in the dark and when under duress. However, if you are in an unfamiliar room and cannot undo the catches, you may have no option but to break the glass. Double-glazed window units, or those with strengthened anti-burglar glass, will not break easily. (If you have windows of this kind, it might make sense to mount a safety hammer on the window frame in case the key cannot be found in an emergency.)

Be aware of glass shards, and wrap your arm with thick clothing for protection. If no hammer is available to break the glass, a small and heavy hard object, such as a bedside lamp or a metal ornament, can be used; if you put

ESCAPING FROM A BUILDING

1 If you are trapped in a room and cannot open a window, put a heavy object in a pillowcase or a sock and use it as a hammer to shatter the glass.

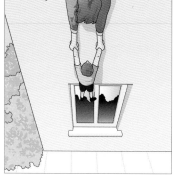

2 To reduce the severity of injuries, the strongest person should lower the lighter occupants from upper windows, rather than letting them jump out.

3 As the last one out, you should lower yourself from the ledge to reduce your fall, remembering to bend the knees before impact then go into a roll.

1 If using an improvised rope to escape, such as knotted sheets or garments, tie it securely to an immovable object that will bear your weight.

2 If no structural anchor points are available, a strong bed frame can be effective as it is too large to be pulled through the window.

3 Grip the improvised rope between your insteps and use arm-over-arm movements to descend quickly – even a short rope will reduce your fall.

PARATROOPER ROLL

1 This roll was devised to prevent injury when hitting hard ground at speed, and it is easy to learn. The legs must be slightly bent at knees and hips.

2 As you hit the ground, absorb the initial impact through your bent legs then roll over on to your thigh and shoulder, swinging the legs over.

3 Keeping the knees and heels together and the lead arm tucked in will spread the impact of the fall throughout the body, saving your ankles and legs.

REVERSE BREAK ROLL

1 If you have no lateral speed, you will take the full-on impact with your legs. You must convert this force into rotational energy before it impacts your spine. Keep your legs bent before impact.

2 Immediately roll backwards as your legs compress, and strike the ground as hard as you can with your arms. This reduces the impact to your spine and adds to your rotational momentum.

3 Make sure you are rolling backwards and not simply falling flat on your back. Continue to roll over backwards. This is the safest and least impactful way to absorb the energy of the fall.

this inside a pillowcase and swing it around your head first, the striking power can be increased markedly.

Escape from ground floor room windows is pretty straightforward, and even from those on the floor above the drop should not kill you unless you fall on your head or land on sharp objects, such as spiked railings.

ESCAPING FROM UPPER FLOORS

Do not just stand on a ledge and jump, but try to find a way of lowering yourself gently. To break your fall, push a mattress out through the window if possible, followed by bedding and anything else that will cushion your fall. When it looks likely that staying in the room will be more hazardous than

risking the fall, drop children and the infirm out of the window, sliding them out feet first and lowering them as far as possible by the wrists before letting go directly over the improvised cushioning.

Ideally, a knotted escape rope or rope ladder should be available if the window is two storeys above ground floor, but few householders give much thought to providing these. An alternative would be to make an improvised rope by knotting sheets or other suitable items together to stretch from window to ground, but this is not a particularly quick fix. If you do have time to do it, make sure you tie the rope to something that will bear your weight. If necessary, push the bed in

front of the window: as it is wider than the frame, it should provide an anchor. Never attempt to jump from a high rise building. You will not survive the fall.

GETTING DOWN STAIRS

If escape through a window is not feasible, and the smoke-filled staircase is the only option, a well-soaked jacket with sleeves tied at the bottom will retain pockets of breathable air. Any remaining oxygen in the corridors and on staircases will be at ground level or close to the steps, so keep low and move slowly. Running fast and upright will probably cause you to inhale poisonous and damaging gases, but taking time without dallying will help conserve your breath.

Emergency home shelter

If a natural disaster hit your area, or your town was suddenly on the frontline of a combat zone, or if international terrorism unleashed a weapon of mass destruction on your doorstep, could you shelter and feed yourself and your family until normality returned?

An ordinary house will keep you safe from the elements in the depth of winter, but when shells and bombs start exploding all around, or if terrorists detonate a "dirty" bomb to contaminate your town, it won't hold up particularly well. However, if you had a strongpoint in the most structurally sound part of the house, and could retreat there with stocks of food and water, you and your loved ones might just make it through. Unless warring forces were to dig in for a battle of attrition, the fighting would probably pass you by

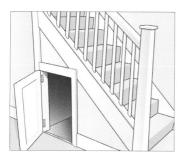

▶ *Maintain a plentiful stock of candles and matches in case the power supply is cut off during an emergency.*

quite quickly, and the contamination caused by a terrorist attack could be even shorter lived, so the ability to build a basic shelter and the availability of enough emergency supplies to last you just a few weeks, could enable you to survive.

SELECTING A SURVIVAL SPACE

In a conventional two- or three-floor urban home, the space beneath the stairs usually offers the best structural protection. In the case of a bombardment, this can be reinforced by removing the internal doors from their hinges and nailing them over the stair treads. The space under the stairs will be cramped and claustrophobic, but unless the house takes a direct hit, it should provide adequate shelter. Line the floor, and the walls where possible, with mattresses and you will have a snug refuge.

Apartment dwellers will probably not have the luxury of an under-stairs cupboard, so they will have to identify the room that seems structurally the strongest, preferably one without windows, in which to build a shelter. Tables sited in the corner of the room, with doors and mattresses on top and on the open sides, can be used to construct a compact refuge, but only if the table legs are

▲ *Terrorist attacks have led manufacturers to produce inexpensive emergency escape masks and smoke hoods for the general public.*

strong enough to take the weight. If they are not, lean the doors against the wall at an angle of more than 45 degrees to give a triangular shelter, and stack mattresses on top for additional protection.

EMERGENCY SUPPLIES

There is no point in having an emergency shelter in your home unless you also have the basics to support life for days, if not weeks. The one

---

IMPROVISED SHELTERS

▲ *The strongest part of many houses is the space under the stairs. It may be cramped and too small for long-term use, but it could save your life.*

▲ *A windowless bathroom can provide a safe retreat in a crisis and is easy to seal against gas attack. Fill the bath with water in case the supply is cut.*

▲ *Failing any other shelter, a mattress and doors stacked around a sturdy table make a survival capsule that offers some protection from explosion and shrapnel.*

▲ *Hosiery secured with a rubber band over the filter tap or stop-cock will act as a makeshift filter for some pollutants.*

constraining factor in assembling your supplies will be storage space. If you are lucky enough to be using a large cellar as your shelter, stocking it with supplies for several weeks will not be a problem.

Water is the primary concern, as humans cannot live for much more than three or four days without water, but if the water is contaminated it could be a double-edged sword. It makes sense to keep at least a few days' supply in large sealed containers in

▼ *Set aside an area in your house or garage for the non-perishable foods and other supplies that will be your go-to in the event of a medium- or long-term supply chain breakdown. Keep it tidy and organized so that you can see at a glance what you have. If you tap into these supplies to cover a non-emergency shortfall, make sure you replace them as soon as possible.*

your shelter all the time, with plenty of empty ones ready to be filled in a crisis and before the supply is cut off. Water filters and/or purification tablets should also be stocked in case the crisis lasts longer than expected. A "volcano" kettle in which to boil water efficiently will also come in handy, as will candles for light; candles also provide a little bit of warmth and can be used to heat canned food. A wind-up radio and torch, which do not need batteries, are also useful to have in your shelter. In a civil defence scenario, radio will be used by the authorities as the primary method of broadcasting information about the emergency.

Adequate stocks of foodstuffs that don't deteriorate are also a necessity, in or close to your shelter. Canned meat, fish and beans, which can be eaten without preparation, are far preferable to dried foodstuffs that will need scarce fuel and water for reconstitution, but dried soups are cheap and use up little storage space and they can perk up the spirits by providing a warm drink when you are cold and downhearted.

If there is a threat of nuclear or biological contamination, temporarily tape up doors, windows and ventilators to the room in which your shelter is located, but remember that you will exhaust your air supply very quickly. When a candle flame starts to die, you will have to pull back the tape and take your chances.

▲ *In an emergency, the radio will be the primary method used by the authorities to inform the public: if you don't have a wind-up radio, stock up with spare batteries.*

HOME SURVIVAL ESSENTIALS

- Drinking water
- Canned food, or other food that does not need cooking or refrigeration
- Can opener
- Candles
- Matches
- Cooker or kettle
- Wind-up radio
- Wind-up torch (flashlight)
- First-aid kit and any essential medication
- Covered bucket
- Clothing and blankets

▼ *Ordinary duct tape is adequate for sealing around doors and windows to protect against chemical or biological agents.*

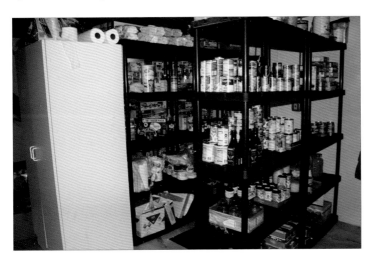

SURVIVING TERRORISM AND CONFLICT

The terrorist strikes out of the blue, when least expected, and almost invariably anonymously. He or she seldom wears a uniform and often plants a bomb and sneaks away before either a timer or remote signal triggers devastation. Even more deadly and effective is the increasingly prevalent, fanatically driven suicide bomber, a development which calls for even more alertness and vigilance in public places and spaces.

Being street smart

Terrorism is usually defined as being the unlawful use of, or the threatened use of, violence against the state or the general public as a politically motivated means of coercion. The 11 September 2001 terrorist attack by Al Qa'eda on the World Trade Center and Pentagon has had a marked affect on both American perceptions of international terrorism and the face of global politics, with the subsequent invasions of Afghanistan and Iraq being just the tip of the iceberg in what President George W. Bush labelled the "War Against Terror". Although 9/11 is seen as the ultimate terrorist act, terrorism is not of course a recent phenomenom. Many countries have now been victim to prolonged and indiscriminate terror attacks from separatist movements within their own country. Elsewhere over the last four or so decades, those seeking to overthrow the state have used the bomb and gun as political tools.

Inevitably, it is the innocent civilian who pays the price. Western holiday destination spots have also become bombers' targets and there are obvious considerations to be made when planning a vacation – not least checking with government alerts.

SUICIDE BOMBERS
While the United Nations tries to agree on a definition of "terrorism", city dwellers have to go on living with the real and present danger of the bomber strapped with explosives or carrying them in a backpack walking into the crowd, martyring themselves and taking countless innocent lives with them. Survival against this type of terrorist is not easy, should you be unlucky enough to cross their path, but if you have good powers of observation and are alert to the tell-tale signals, you may just survive.

Bombs, or to be more precise improvised explosive devices, are favoured methods of terror delivery. (Kidnappings and hostage-taking are also part of their arsenal and these are

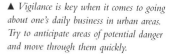

dealt with on later pages.) In times of heightened tension, government offices, military establishments, recruitment offices, power and water supply networks, airports and stations all become terrorist targets, and should be avoided where possible.

Anniversaries that are in some way related to the separatists' struggle are obvious magnets for those wishing to either heighten awareness of their cause, or to create fear and outrage among the public; the 1987 IRA bomb attack on a Remembrance Sunday

▲ *Vigilance is key when it comes to going about one's daily business in urban areas. Try to anticipate areas of potential danger and move through them quickly.*

service in Enniskillen, which killed 11 and injured more than 60, being just one example of the latter. Through simply being aware of places where and times when the terrorist might be tempted to attack, and altering your plans to avoid these, you greatly reduce your chances of being caught up in such terrorist actions.

▲ *CCTV and identity cards will not stop the fanatical terrorist but they can help identify suspects in public areas.*

▲ *Police around the world are armed now as a matter of routine which makes lethal outcomes more likely.*

▶ *Public spaces such as rail terminals are obvious targets for indiscriminate terrorist activity and you need to use your powers of observation to spot anything suspicious.*

PUBLIC AWARENESS

Could the Madrid railway bombings of March 2004 have been foreseen? With Spain's support for the Coalition invasion of Iraq in March 2003 and the chance to sway the result of forthcoming elections, the populace and the authorities should have been on heightened alert. More to the point, those in the carriages where the bombs were left unattended in luggage might have realized the potential danger and taken action before it was too late.

On 7 July 2005, after a four-year respite from terrorist bombings, due to the changed political climate in Northern Ireland, London was plunged back into chaos by a series of suicide bombs. This was a tactic never seen before in Britain – though it had been anticipated – and one that is harder to both detect and foil. This time the bombers did not leave unattended packages, but stayed with their lethal devices, dying in the blast themselves. They escaped detection by not standing out. Over 50 innocent civilians died after three bombs, carried in rucksacks, were detonated almost simultaneously in the cramped confines of under-ground railway carriages across the capital, and a fourth exploded on a city centre bus just under an hour later. At the time Britain was hosting the G8 international political summit, ensuring maximum attention for the terrorists' cause. Two weeks later an unsuccessful copycat attack failed.

WHAT YOU CAN DO

Be street smart. Use your powers of deduction and observational skills to keep you alert to possible terrorist dangers, blending in with your surroundings. What police and military close-protection and undercover operatives dub "playing the grey man", is one of the most important skills to master. If the terrorist can neither single you as a potential target nor mark you out as deserving special attention, your chances of survival increase dramatically. Don't stand out. Don't be the hero. Don't switch off to your surroundings. It is probably only you that holds the key to personal survival in a terrorism setting.

SEARCHING FOR CAR BOMBS

1 Check the wheel arches and around the underside where a sandwich box-sized device can be concealed. Memorize what the underside of your car looks like.

2 Check for signs of tampering – such as a forced door or marks or damage around the lock – and peek inside the interior for anything out of place.

3 A mirror on a pole (with a torch attached for checking in the dark), either improvised or a bought one, will help you see into vehicle recesses.

4 Do not assume that just because you cannot see a foreign object under your vehicle it is safe. Before opening the door, check the interior.

Being taken prisoner or hostage

In the past few decades there have been cases of aid workers and contractors being kidnapped whilst at work and this is increasingly becoming a method used by certain terrorist groups to publicize their cause. It is extremely difficult to always protect foreign nationals in high-risk countries. To the committed terrorist, seizing an innocent charity worker is a sure way to attract the attention of the international media and in recent years terrorist organizations have shown themselves to have very little or no regard for human life. If you are taken hostage by a terrorist group the situation is extremely grave.

A kidnap for ransom is big business for criminals with or without political leanings. To the gangster, a foreign businessman or engineer employed by a wealthy company can be just as tempting a target as someone who works for a bank vault.

Terrorists and criminals or, to be more specific, their foot soldiers, are not always the most logical or intelligent of people, so you do not need to belong to a high-risk group to be a potential kidnap victim. Mistakes of identity are easily made, or not even worried about, so it is essential that you try at the very least not to look like a vulnerable

target, and also that you take basic precautions to make it harder for kidnappers to seize you. Once again, become the grey man or woman so that you do not stand out from the crowd, and keep your wits about you for potential danger.

EARLIEST ESCAPE ESSENTIAL

If you are taken prisoner, you must attempt to escape at the earliest opportunity. The longer your captors have you, the less your chances are of getting away from them. During the initial lift, you will most likely be simply bundled into a vehicle by one

KIDNAP SCENARIO

1 Those who work with large sums of cash, such as bank employees and payroll staff, and their families, can be potential robbery kidnap victims.

2 If kidnapped outside of the home, a get-away will be needed for the victim. Unless death or serious injury seems likely, try not to go quietly and easily.

3 The best time to escape captivity is immediately on capture while everything is still fluid and out in the open. Seize any opportunity you can.

4 If your captors are distracted, hit out and run. At this stage you are probably too valuable for them to seriously hurt you. Try to escape being incarcerated.

5 Once you know there is no chance of escape, try to befriend and take an interest in your captors. Such bonding might save your life.

6 When your captors are in total control, be submissive to survive; don't be confrontational. Bide your time until an escape plan presents itself.

or two assailants and driven speedily away. Unless you are very switched-on, this part of the operation will pass in a blur, but it offers your first chance of escape. As they throw or drag you through one door, try to use your momentum and the power of your limbs to burst out of the opposite door – the chances are that it will be unlocked so that the team can make a quick escape if they run into trouble during the pick-up.

A van offers better rear-door options. Try to burst out through the rear doors as soon as you are lifted, as a broken shoulder and a few cracked ribs are a better option than captivity or worse. To avoid injury, try to work out which door of the two opens first before you hit the other one and find that it is secured in such a way that it is impossible to budge.

BUNDLED INTO THE BOOT

Up to now, we have assumed that you are conscious when thrown into the vehicle and that your captors are merely planning on hooding, gagging and binding you once they have you in the back. If they knock you out during the pick-up, it is likely that you will already be tightly bound and gagged by the time you come around, but if they merely throw you into the boot or trunk of a saloon, you may still have a chance. Your captors will have needed to use quite a large car for the boot to be big enough to fit an adult in speedily, and these days most large cars have a cable release to let the driver pop it open from the inside, so look around quickly to see if you can detect such a device running into the inner lock mechanism.

If there is no cable release, it may also be possible to spring the lock from the inside using a tyre lever or even the pressed metal stand for a warning triangle to pry the jaws apart. Chances are that either of these, which are carried as standard in many countries, could be stowed on brackets or in compartments to keep them out of the way and out of view when not needed. Hopefully your kidnappers have not spotted them either.

ESCAPING A LOCKED CAR

1 If you have to kick out a safety glass windscreen, remember the glass won't fall out or separate into pieces. It's held together by laminated plastic layers.

2 To kick out a broken windscreen in one piece brace yourself against the seat. Use a bag, coat or book to protect your feet as your legs strike through the glass.

3 Strike any of the other windows with a hard metal object near the edge of the glass. They will smash quite easily. Avert your eyes or cover them.

4 Clean off the broken shards from the edges of the frame with your chosen tool to avoid serious injury while you are making your escape.

JUMPING ON THE MOVE

If you really believe your life is in peril and the vehicle is speeding away, you will have to jump while travelling at speed. First try to pull the handbrake before opening the door suddenly and pushing yourself out at an angle away from the direction of the car. You will be moving at the same speed as the car so jump where you think you can hit grass or soft ground or undergrowth. Protect your head as much as possible by wrapping your arms around it and keep rolling away in a tucked-in position. (Try to adopt the Paratrooper Roll position shown on page 103.) If you have escaped injury get away fast to avoid re-capture by zig-zagging between any parked vehicles and buildings.

Warning: This is an extremely dangerous manoeuvre and should only be attempted in a truly life-threatening situation.

IF TAKEN HOSTAGE

- Keep calm – your captors will be in a highly emotional state and the situation will be very volatile.
- Don't become aggressive.
- Reassure others if they are showing signs of strain.
- Make yourself useful to your captors as much as possible by helping with other hostages.
- Get rid of any documents that may make the captors single you out.
- Keep your mind alert and look for chances to escape all the time.
- Listen to your captors grievances – don't try to argue politics.
- Talk about your family and show pictures if possible to make yourself more of an individual and less of a victim.

Survival in captivity

Once your captors have brought you to the place where they intend to hold you captive, possibly the first of many places that will be used, your chances of escape will diminish considerably. Here, unlike while they have you in transit, they will be in complete control of you and will no doubt have done their best to ensure that escape is difficult, if not impossible. That does not mean that they will not have made mistakes, and you will probably now have plenty of time to allow your brain to work out where they may have gone wrong, but unless you think that you are worth no more to them alive than dead, it is probably still well worth trying to make a run for it at the earliest opportunity.

EARLIEST ESCAPE ATTEMPT

By making an early escape attempt, you will not only test the resolve of your captors, but may well glean additional information for future attempts. On the other hand, you are likely to receive blows in return at best, or a severe beating at worst. Only you will know if you have the strength of will to take this. Just remember that every bit of information that you gain on the routine of your captors and the layout outside your immediate prison, could

▼ *When left on your own, explore all possible escape routes. Try to find a potential way out that can be concealed while you are working on it.*

▲ *Conventional handcuffs are not easy to escape from, but with practice you should be able to slip your hands over your posterior to bring them to the front of the body.*

▲ *Make use of your observational skills to identify captor routines and spot potential escape routes or methods. Don't merely wait for rescue, as it may not come.*

affect how and when you eventually escape. If the room outside your prison door is living accommodation for a large group of armed men, chances are that you will not be going out that way, but if there is only one guard sitting on a chair outside the door and you determine that there is a door or window to the outside world in the room or corridor, you could well be onto an escape route.

▼ *Always check the obvious. Don't assume that just because a window has a lock, that it is functional, or that it cannot be forced to give a quiet and simple escape route.*

GAINING THEIR SYMPATHY

Let's assume that you are of some worth, be that political or financial, to your captors and that they have no reason to torture you for information or pleasure. Ideologically and culturally you could be worlds apart, but your jailers are still human beings, so you should try to find ways of gaining their sympathy and even bonding with them. Anything that will make your life in captivity easier or increase the chances of you escaping should be tried. Do not assume that your government or employer will pay a ransom or make political concessions to those holding you captive, as to do so would be seen as a sign of weakness and would just lead to more kidnappings. Do not bank on anyone coming to your rescue for a long time, if ever, as you will almost certainly be on your own.

MENTAL AND PHYSICAL TOOLS

Prepare yourself mentally for a long and boring wait, but use your time wisely to find a way out of your predicament. Remember that your mind is the one place that the kidnappers cannot inhabit. To describe every potential way of escaping from a room would take a whole book, and

NYLON CABLE TIES

These days, it is likely that your captor will use cable ties to bind you as they are light and easy to use. They bind the wrists and ankles tighter than cord, are near impossible to break, and cut into the skin if you struggle. You can loosen them by releasing the ratchet lock, but you'll need an accomplice or a utensil to do so. You can break them by placing your palms together, arms above your head, and then striking the hands downwards, fingers pointing up, and elbows moving out to the sides so that as your fingers are forced together your palms pry your wrists apart. With luck, the ties will break as they pass your navel. It takes speed and strength and is incredibly painful. Your energy might be better spent finding something to cut them – rough stone or metal, a door hinge or similar. Or your hidden razor blade.

most methods would be of little relevance to your particular situation. That you are reading this book suggests that you are interested enough to have read many news reports where actual escapes were mentioned, and you are bound to have seen films where the hero or heroine breaks out from incarceration. Use your mind to draw parallels with your current predicament and discover that chink in their armour that will rid you of your captors.

HOSTAGE SITUATIONS

Terrorism is usually behind most hostage situations, though occasionally a bank robbery may go wrong and the crooks decide to use those in the building as bargaining tools. Either way, if caught up in a situation like this you will be faced with dangerous and possibly unstable captors. As with a kidnapping, grab any opportunity to escape in the initial confusion, but if that is not possible you must try to keep alert.

If your captors are negotiating with the authorities for either political

concessions or the opportunity to escape themselves, there may be times when it is in their interest to release captives. The obvious ones in such a situation are children, women, the aged and the infirm. If you can, convince your captors that you are ill by feigning the symptoms of heart trouble or food poisoning or missing your medication. The last thing captors need if using hostages as a bargaining tool are dead or dying prisoners, so if you act convincingly you might just get away with it.

Play the sympathy card in terms of "understanding" their cause and listen to their grievances. It is often the best way of getting past their guard.

If your captors are terrorists and you belong to a religious or national grouping that they consider to be the enemy, you must try to mask this. Simple things like adopting a fake accent to hide your English or American one could be enough to throw them off the scent. It is the inconspicuous hostage that is most likely to survive.

BOUND AND TIED

▲ If rope is used to secure your wrists, you have a good chance of loosening and untying it. Tense your fists to gain a degree of looseness.

▲ Given time alone, and with your hands brought to the front for access, ropes can be loosened further and knots unpicked by using your teeth.

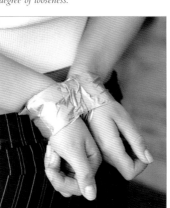

▲ Broad fabric, electrical or gaffa tape is stronger than rope when in tension and if twisted, but carefully nick the edge first and you might tear it laterally.

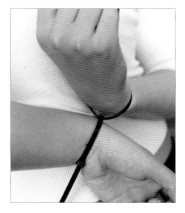

▲ A pair of nylon ties is the worst wrist binding to escape from as the nylon cuts into the flesh when put under tension. They need to be cut or broken.

Transport hijacks

Planes, coaches and trains pose an obvious target for terrorists as they provide large numbers of hostages packed into a small, mobile and controllable area. With the notable exception of the 9/11 attack on the World Trade Center and the Pentagon, where the terrorists killed themselves and everyone else on board the aircraft, almost every transport hijack has seen captives being taken primarily for publicity purposes, with most eventually being either released or rescued. However, with an increase in the use of suicide bombers by terrorist organizations, and the willingness of those bombers to take the lives of their captives at the same time, one can no longer afford to just sit back and wait for someone else to come to the rescue. Any chance to escape must be seized if you want to survive.

SKYJACKING

Escape from an aircraft in flight is virtually impossible, so if it is clear that the hijackers intend taking your and their lives at some point, you have absolutely nothing to lose in attempting to overpower them. This is exactly what happened on Flight 93, the fourth aircraft hijacked on 11 September 2001, and although those who struck out against the terrorists did not succeed in turning the tables, their

heroic attempt did prevent the hijacked aircraft from reaching its intended target and taking countless more lives.

If you are caught up in such a situation, you will have to identify fellow passengers both mentally and physically fit enough to back you up and positioned in the aircraft where they can help you take out all captors at the same time. On many scheduled flights these days, there will be at least one sky marshal aboard, but the hijackers may well have identified and neutralized him or her, so don't bank on help from that direction.

▲ *High value performance cars and expensive 4 x 4 SUVs make attractive targets for thieves, who may wait for the owner to appear with the keys, then attack.*

If you find yourself in need of a self-defence weapon aboard, you will need to have identified cabin fittings or items of passenger baggage that could be used. Anything around you – from a handbag or camera strap, which could be a replacement for rope, to bits of aircraft trim that could be turned into improvised cutting tools or weapons – should be identified; even that bottle of

---

CARJACK ESCAPE

1 A hooded criminal with a weapon climbs into the passenger seat and attempts to carjack your car with you in the driving seat. Think quickly.

2 As the driver, you are actually in control. When travelling at a reasonable speed release his belt, if he is wearing one, and step violently on the brakes.

3 Taken by surprise, he should either hit the dashboard or be temporarily incapacitated by the air bag, and you can exit the vehicle quickly.

▲ *An evocative memorial near Shanksville, Pennsylvania, USA, where Flight 93 crashed on 11 September 2001. A National Memorial is being built there to honour the dead. The 40 passengers learned on mobile phones that they were one of four suicide attacks. They decided to fight and nearly succeeded in overcoming their captors.*

▲ *A "close protection" team practises ambush drills on a live-fire range. A high value business target or a contractor working in a conflict zone may need their services.*

▼ *In a "close protection" situation, your bodyguards will run you through possible scenarios and evasive action drills. Pay close attention if you wish to survive.*

duty free spirits could become a cosh in an emergency. When life or death situations arise, necessity is the mother of invention.

LIKELY SCENARIOS

In most cases the hijackers will gather all captives in one large group, usually at the back of the aircraft, coach or railway carriage, where they pose less threat of coming to the aid of the pilot or driver. Due to the close confines and high seat backs, this could work to your favour by allowing you to communicate with fellow plotters. When you are moved you may have the chance to secure an aisle seat from where you can launch your attempt to overpower the hijackers – assuming that you didn't get the chance to do so during the move itself. Try to stay alert at all times to any opportunities.

Once the aircraft is on the ground, or the coach or train is stationary, it makes sense to try to make a mad dash for freedom as soon as you can. Unless you have loved ones on board, make your move. If you can get to an emergency escape door and open it (instructions are on that aircraft seat pocket card that nobody bothers to read), a broken ankle or two caused by the jump to freedom might just save

your life, and if you roll under the aircraft fuselage when you hit the ground, the hijackers won't be able to shoot you. Escape from a coach or train can be easier, as a sharp hit on the glazing with an escape hammer or any other suitable heavy pointed implement, will give you instant access to the outside world – you just have to be quick and fit enough to take the opportunity when it presents itself.

The most dangerous time for hostages held captive in any mode of transport is the moment when the

security forces try to effect a release, as the smoke, stun bombs and panic bring on a tirade of lethal bullets, while the terrorists may also decide to trigger explosive devices.

If you see your captor is about to trigger explosives, tackling him or her might just be your only chance of survival. However, if this is not an apparent risk try to keep alert, look out for the security forces and their instructions, keep still and avoid any sudden movement that could attract shots in your direction.

Bombs and explosives

The bomb, be it placed in a car, a waste bin, an abandoned suitcase, or strapped to a fanatic's body, is the classic terrorist weapon. Unfortunately, if you happen to be at the wrong place at the wrong time and get caught up in an bomb attack, your survival will very much be determined by where you are sitting or standing at the time impact. Bombers usually strike with little or no warning, or worse, they give a warning that is actually intended to drive victims into the killing zone of the weapon of mass terror.

BEING FOREWARNED

The only ways to guarantee survival from bomb attacks are to be aware of potential targets and therefore avoid them, and to be constantly alert for suspicious packages and individuals. In metropolitan cities the world over police, soldiers and security guards are trained to watch for suspicious signs that could identify a bomber as he or she approaches. Either excess shiftiness and heavy sweating, or a state of euphoria, can betray the potential suicide vest wearer, but so too can the more obvious visual clues such as an excessively bulky torso when the rest of the person is conventionally proportioned. Many security personnel have lost their lives by spotting a bomber before they reached the intended target and forcing an early trigger, thereby saving countless other innocent lives by their sacrifice.

The suitcase or sports bag bomb, left in an airport, railway station, coach station or even aboard a railway train, is the classic low-risk but high-casualty weapon used by terrorists around the globe. Observation, and avoiding the places where such bombs may be left, are the keys to survival in such cases. If you see unattended luggage or a suspicious package on public transport or in airport or station terminal rest room, give it as wide a berth as possible and report it to someone in authority.

Never, ever, move it or open it to see what is inside, as the clued-up bomb

maker will almost certainly have built in some form of anti-handling device that will automatically detonate it.

MOVE ON TO SAFETY ZONES

We cannot avoid being in places that the terrorist may choose as a target, but we can certainly increase our chances of survival by passing through as quickly as possible. At airports, for example, check in early to avoid queues and the need to loiter on the public side. Once you have checked in your hold baggage, move straight through to the departure lounge, where all hand luggage will have been security screened and the chances of a terrorist incident are reduced.

THE DANGER OF FLYING GLASS

In a bomb blast away from the epicentre the vast majority of injuries are caused by flying shards of glass. If you have to spend any length of time in an area at high risk of bomb attack, try to keep well clear of windows and large glazed areas. Normally it is best to position yourself in a corner, facing entrances or doors, from where you can observe everything that is going on around you. However, if you feel exposed and vulnerable, particularly if there is a lot of glazing around, sit with your back towards the potential threat

▲ *The UK has had considerable experience of dealing with modern terrorist attacks for many decades.*

area so that at least your eyes are protected, as they are the part of you most likely to be severely injured if on the periphery of the blast area.

▼ *A few sticks of explosive in a backpack – self-detonated or activated by a timing device – is an increasingly common weapon in terrorist activity.*

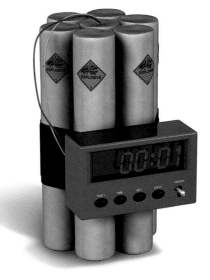

▶ *In the event of a blast, cover your mouth and nose as emergency protection and get out of the vicinity fast, as another blast might be detonated.*

▲ *Discreetly armoured cars like this Range Rover afford good protection against bullet and blast, but they cost a small fortune.*

▲ *If you spot a suspicious package or case on a train, don't touch it. Call the authorities and don't be afraid to halt the service.*

SECONDARY DETONATIONS

Very often an initial bomb attack will be followed up with a second blast either to blow up security forces responding to the incident, or kill and maim those innocent bystanders or personnel who are now gathered around the crime scene. Should you be caught up in a terrorist bomb attack, don't hang around on the periphery or allow yourself to be corralled into a holding area. Get as far away from the scene as you can, as fast as possible, keeping your wits about you and your eyes peeled for follow-up attacks.

▲ *The world's underground train systems are particularly vulnerable to terrorist attack. Stay alert and report anything unusual.*

IF A BOMB GOES OFF

1 In the event of a blast away from the epicentre, turn away immediately to protect your eyes and vital organs from flying glass and shrapnel.

2 Throw yourself flat on the floor with your head away from the seat of the blast as shrapnel tends to spread out in an upwards direction.

3 Use your arms to protect your highly vulnerable ears and eyes (the aircraft safety position) if trapped in a confined space with a bomb.

Toxic gases and poisons

In the early 2000s the spectre of Weapons of Mass Destruction (WMD) in Iraq brought the subject of toxic gases, biochemical weapons and other poisons into the public eye, but these nasties had actually been around for the best part of a century. During World War I between 1914 and 1918, both sides used and suffered from poison gas attacks, but in the main these were not used against civilian targets. Then, in the late 1980s, when Saddam Hussein wiped out the population of a Kurdish town in a chemical attack, the topic came into the public eye. During the Iran–Iraq war in the 1980s, both sides had claimed that the other used chemical weapons on the battlefield but, just like with the war itself, few outside the region paid much attention.

It was only when Saddam invaded Kuwait in 1990 that the international community started to panic about the chemical and biological weapons that they believed he was capable of using. This fear rumbled on through the last decade of the 20th century, and when the predominantly Anglo-American

▼ *Specialist decontamination units should eventually take care of any survivors.*

invasion of Iraq took place in 2003, it was the neutralizing of the WMD that was cited as being the driving force. It has now been admitted that no WMD have been found in Iraq, though the fear is that they or their constituent parts may have fallen into the hands of terrorists.

The same can be said for missing stocks of chemicals from the defunct Warsaw Pact days, and periodically the

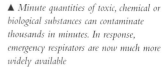

▲ *Minute quantities of toxic, chemical or biological substances can contaminate thousands in minutes. In response, emergency respirators are now much more widely available*

mass media in Europe and America runs a scare story on this. The only major use of this type of weapon in a terror attack was when a Japanese religious sect released a quantity of sarin nerve gas on the Tokyo subway in 1995, killing 12 people and affecting over 5,000 others. The chemical used in this incident turned out to be an impure strain which the group had manufactured themselves.

DEADLY AND INVISIBLE AGENTS
Chemical and biological agents of the type likely to be used by terrorists cannot easily be detected before they affect you, and normally the first symptoms are breathing difficulties or vision problems. The one thing which might just save you is the immediate donning of a respirator when you see others beginning to be affected, but even then, there is no guarantee that your model will be proof against the threat, as each chemical or biological agent has its own individual

▲ *A decontamination team moves into action. The threat of chemical or biological attack by terrorists is very real.*

▲ *A trauma victim (role player) in the aftermath of a terrorist attack.*

characteristics and general purpose masks can only guard against a limited range. However, any protection has to be better than none.

EMERGENCY RESPIRATORS

Since the outbreak of suspected anthrax attacks in the USA following the 9/11 terrorist outrage in New York, Washington and Pennsylvania, and a heightened awareness of how easily terrorists could obtain or manufacture basic chemical or biological weapons, relatively affordable pocket-sized emergency respirators have become available for civilian purchase. As

competition kicks in their price is dropping. If you are a regular passenger on mass transit systems, or if you frequent large public indoor events that could possibly be a tempting target for the terrorist, carrying one of these lightweight masks makes sense.

Some extremist political activist groups, seeking everything from regime change to the stopping of fur wearing or the performing of abortions, have turned away from the letter bomb to the chemical terror attack through the post. Usually some form of odourless powder is used, as sending liquids by mail is much harder. In almost every case, terrorist attacks like these turn out to be well-prepared hoaxes.

Government advice to anyone who may be a possible target for chemical

attack, or who deals with mail in a high-risk industry, is simply to be aware, to not disturb and to clean up afterwards. Awareness of suspicious packages is the first priority, followed by gently opening all mail, with an opener rather than fingers, in a manner that will not disturb the contents.

Once the package is open, preferably on a clear flat surface, do not shake or pour out the contents, nor should one blow into the envelope, as airborne contamination can be the killer. Finally, it's important to clean your hands after dealing with mail, as the second most common form of chemical poisoning is ingestion through the skin.

▼ *Should you fall victim to a chemical or biological attack with no protection to wear, get out into the open as quickly as possible, and fight the urge to panic.*

▼ *By keeping upwind of others who have become contaminated, you will reduce the chances of inhaling or ingesting more poison. But a mask is a must to survive longer term.*

▼ *Attempting to wash off any contaminant – fire hoses are the obvious choice at public venues – will lessen its effects and prolong your chances of survival.*

War zones

Since the end of the Cold War, when the political balance between the American and Soviet superpowers broke down, the world has become a much more unstable place. A conflict can flare up anywhere in the world when centuries-old hatred boils to the surface and civil war breaks out between neighbours who have lived in harmony for decades and are now pitted against one another in the ultimate battle for survival. Most people think of war as being waged by one government upon another, but in reality it is more often ethnic or religious differences that bring about wars, many being civil wars rather than wars between nations.

WAR ZONE SURVIVAL
Survival in a war zone, where you not only have to avoid the enemy but also battle against mother nature when the infrastructure collapses around you, depends primarily on three basics:
• You must have the abilities to adapt as conditions deteriorate around you.

▼ *As thunder follows lightning, so a blast and shockwave will follow the initial explosive flash, so keep down and brace yourself.*

• You need to be able to construct a refuge that you and your loved ones can retreat to, certainly for days and maybe for weeks on end as the battlefront hopefully passes by.
• You have to build and maintain stocks of water, food and essentials to get you through the hardest times. The very fact that you are reading this book probably means that you are probably someone with a grasp of that first basic – the ability to adapt.

▲ *Ship and ferry hijacks are on the increase. Here special forces recapture a hijacked ship during a maritime counter-terrorism exercise.*

WAR ON YOUR DOORSTEP
While there will be some who have the ideal base for a refuge in the form of a cellar, the vast majority of the population of the developed world are town or city dwellers and that will probably not be an option. In such circumstances it will be necessary to turn one room, preferably the one with the fewest outer walls and windows, into a refuge with both sleeping accommodation and emergency water and food stocks.

As per the measures described on pages 102–3, a survival cell should be constructed in one part of the room, ideally the one farthest from outside walls and closest to a stairway where the structure will be stronger. You will need to improvise some overhead protection against falling rubble caused by nearby explosions, so under the stairs is a sensible option if there is sufficient space. The survival cell should be your main sleeping area, and it is also where your emergency water and medical supplies should be kept. If the fighting gets close, or if your locality is subject to bomb or artillery attack, you should retreat there immediately.

It is essential that adequate stocks of basic, non-perishable foodstuffs are stocked in your refuge, but stocks of drinking water are more important. The human body is remarkably resilient and can survive for weeks on little or no food, but without drinking water you will last only a few days.

In towns and cities, the two first major casualties of war tend to be power supplies and piped water, mainly because power stations are key targets for attackers, and the water supply relies on electricity to pump it out to homes and businesses. Limited emergency water can be kept in the bath, protected by a tarpaulin or board, but even if you seal around the plug with silicone before filling it to avoid any leakage, one bath of water is unlikely to last for long. As time passes you will have to use precious fuel supplies to boil the water to ensure it is still safe to drink. Maintaining stocks of bottled drinking water, preferably in 50-litre plastic containers or larger, is a good idea.

It is also sensible to maintain a large stock of basic long-life foodstuffs in your refuge, especially high-protein

▼ *In addition to constantly training with each other, police and military counter-terrorist teams regularly exchange information and techniques internationally.*

canned meat, fish and beans. Do not be tempted to store too much low-bulk dehydrated foodstuffs, or things like pasta and oats which require water for their preparation, as you will need to use valuable drinking water and fuel to make a meal. In peacetime cold beans or beef stew may not seem too appetizing, but if you are stuck in your survival cell for days at a time, as fighting rages all around, you will look forward with great anticipation to mealtimes of cold canned food. Your state of mind largely depends upon getting enough nutrition, and staying positive is key to successful survival.

▶ *Breathable, warm, windproof and waterproof gear is essential when the power supplies are cut off. A feather-down sleeping bag will provide good insulation.*

▲ *Curfews are commonly set for dusk to dawn so security forces can keep a lid on terrorism or insurgency. You must not go outside at such times as you are putting yourself in unnecessary danger.*

Survival in the workplace

To the terrorist, the commercial world can sometimes be a better target than the civilian population. Society cannot easily function without bureaucracy, banks and big business, so the public servant, bank employee and business executive can easily find themselves in the front line. In recent years every "direct action" group, from animal rights activists and anarchists through to religious fundamentalists, has attacked businesses and the symbols of Western capitalism either to publicize their cause, to create a climate of fear in society at large, or to hammer home their political stance, so the laboratory technician, the office worker and even the counter assistant in the burger bar can also find themselves at risk.

If anarchists are attacking where you work, it is most likely to be during a public order crisis and the assault will probably be overt and aimed primarily at the premises, so your personal survival should not be too much of an issue. Just take off your work uniform and leave quietly by the side entrance. However, if political activists or religious fundamentalists pick on you, the attack is likely to be less overt.

LETTER BOMBS

The letter or parcel bomb and, to a lesser extent, hazardous substances such as toxins or biochemical agents, are the primary method of attack, and must be guarded against if you work for a high-risk commercial or government target.

▲ *The 6m/20ft tall cast iron "cross" found in the rubble of the World Trade Center was adopted by rescue workers as a symbol of faith.*

Usually, it will be the post-room worker or the secretarial assistant who falls victim to these devices, but if you open your own mail you must be aware of the potential threat.

Often bomb or hazardous-substance attacks against businesses involve carefully constructed hoax packages, as the fear of attack is often just as effective as the real thing, and the dangers of losing public sympathy by maiming or killing the wrong victim are less. Even so, the stress and trauma of opening a package and finding it contains a fake bomb or a mysterious powder along with a warning message is not a pleasant experience.

With the spread of the internet since the late 1990s, fanatics with only basic technical skills have been able to learn how to build a cheap improvised explosive device from easily sourced components, so the threat to the public has never been greater. To the anti-vivisectionist attacking pharmaceutical company employees, the political activist attempting to disrupt government departments or even the disgruntled former employee seeking revenge, the bomb delivered by post is

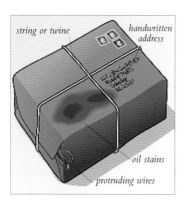

◀ *The parcel bomb has long been a method of attack for separatist and animal rights terrorists. Incorrectly addressed labels, twine bindings or odd bulges can be warning signs.*

string or twine
handwritten address
oil stains
protruding wires

an anonymous and effective weapon. The last thing that most terrorists want is to be traced, so they will try to leave as few clues as possible on the package.

If the address is handwritten – and in most cases it will be as setting up computer-printed address labels can leave incriminating evidence – the writer will almost certainly try to disguise their handwriting, but the human eye and brain can usually easily spot this, so your first line of defence is to read the label. The device will also have been packaged so that it does not go off in transit and it is unlikely to be timer-driven due to the vagaries of the postal system, so handling it unopened should be safe. If it looks suspicious or feels suspicious, simply back off and call in the experts. It is better to be an embarrassed survivor than a dead fool.

LESSONS FROM 9/11

Since 9/11, businesses – especially in high-rise buildings – have taken risk assessment much more seriously with routine "major incident" evacuations and fire drills being timed and assessed. The 9/11 outrage was perpetrated by terrorists, but it could just as easily have been a terrible accident (after all, a B-25 bomber had crashed into the 78th floor of the Empire State Building on 28 July 1945) and it was one which was actually foreseen when the building was originally designed. Back in those days, wide-bodied jets had yet to take to the skies, so the designers underestimated the size of the aircraft that eventually tested their foresight, but even so they provided sufficient means of escape for all survivors beneath the impact-affected floors. What they could not factor in was that some people failed to get out at the first sign of trouble, resulting in them perishing when the towers eventually collapsed.

The Twin Towers had already been the subject of a major bomb attack by the same group, which caused several deaths and badly damaged the lower floors, so people working there

FREEFALL

You sometimes hear that you should jump immediately before an elevator crashes, so you would be "floating" at the second of impact. Chances are your freefall will be slowed by the compression of air at the bottom of the shaft as it fell (like a piston compresses air in a bicycle pump). The air pressure would slow the elevator down. Also many cable elevators have built-in shock absorbers at the bottom of the shaft – to cushion the impact. Either try to cling on to a ledge as shown or lie flat on the floor so that no single part of your body takes the brunt of the blow.

could have realized they were a potential terrorist target. When the first plane struck, with such devastating consequences and igniting several floors, many workers in both the neighbouring tower and on the lower, unaffected floors of the first tower, remained in their offices rather than following the well-documented emergency evacuation plans. Rather than looking to their personal survival, they waited either to be told what to do, or assumed that the emergency services would have the matter in hand.

OFFICE SAFETY

Remember that it is down to you as the individual to make your own risk assessment before trouble strikes, and have a plan to ensure your survival. Just in case that fateful day comes (and bear in mind that we could just as easily be talking of a building fire or a natural disaster as a terrorist attack), you should be well aware of how to get out by both the fastest route and by at least one secondary one should your first choice be unusable. In an emergency, you cannot count on the electricity and lighting supplies being maintained, as back-up systems could well be taken out by the incident, so make sure you know how to escape in the dark as well.

It makes sense to work as close to your emergency escape route as possible, so try to engineer this if at all possible. Time is precious in an

▲ *Check your company has fully implemented evacuation procedures in the event of a terrorist incident.*

emergency situation, and if you have to fight your way through a packed open-plan office with dozens of terrified workmates, you will already be at a disadvantage. If you have a say in the matter, opt for having your workplace near the emergency exit.

By their very nature, internal fire escapes tend to be the strongest parts of buildings, being either in the central core, or at the corners or ends of buildings where they form a self-standing structural feature. This is another good reason to have your workplace sited near them. If a vehicle bomb is used against the building, these are the areas most likely to suffer the least structural damage and subsequent collapse, thereby increasing your chances of survival.

Be aware that after blast trauma, flying glass presents the major injury hazard to most people. Even a bomb exploding several hundred metres away against a totally unrelated target will cause most windows in the vicinity to shatter, with terrifying results. It is tempting to sit near windows, perhaps so that the view will break up the monotony of office life, but should terrorists strike nearby, that view could well be the last thing you see. Consider your desk site, if you have a choice.

SURVIVING ACTS OF NATURE

Nature is unpredictable and awesome. It can threaten us out of the blue, as with a tsunami, which because of its rarity is a complete shock and draws on the most basic of survival instincts. Even in familiar surroundings people are sometimes confronted by a totally unexpected and potentially devastating scenario. In survival terms preparation and attitude are what matter. The topics covered in this chapter are intended to help prepare for such situations.

Natural disasters

Being prepared for an earthquake or hurricane is the best way to survive one. Discuss the possibilities with your family and colleagues so you have a plan if disaster strikes. Always check radio and local area networks (internet) as well for disaster area advice.

EARTHQUAKE
If you are affected by an earthquake, stay calm. Don't run or panic. If you're indoors, stay there. If you are out of doors, remain outside. Most injuries occur as people are entering or exiting buildings. If possible take cover under something that will protect you from being hurt by falling masonry or other building materials or structures – under a table or upturned sofa, or next to a solid wall. Stay away from glass, windows or outside doors. Put out any fires and stay away from utility wires and anything overhead.

If you're in a car, stop carefully and stay in the vehicle until the shaking ceases. It's a good safe place to be. Do not stop on or under a bridge or flyover, nor under overhead cables or street lights. Look out for fallen debris.

▼ Earthquakes can shatter constructed objects as easily as natural ones – don't think you are safe anywhere, but in particular avoid bridges and flyovers.

▲ Looking down into this volcano's crater we can see a low-energy eruption taking place. A column of steam rises high into the air, and hot ash is billowing out, but there is no sign of an explosion or pyroclastics.

VOLCANO
Many volcanos are harmless, described by geologists as either extinct or dormant. However, an active volcano always has the potential to erupt and cause catastrophic damage. Most volcanic eruptions are slow affairs, quite unlike the ferocious explosion on New Zealand's Whakaari/White Island in 2019. Usually the eruption produces only slow-moving rivers of ash or lava and a variety of poisonous gases. That makes them extremely dangerous if you are in their path, but relatively easy to escape from. There is also a more insidious danger from vast quantities of odourless carbon monoxide which can collect in still valleys (or basements) and which can lull you into sleep, followed by oxygen deprivation and death.

Stay away from lava flows even if they seem to have cooled. Move directly away from the volcano and do not shelter in low-lying areas. If a volcano explodes, the land for miles around can be devastated and all landmarks eradicated. You will find yourself stumbling around an unrecognizable, smoking landscape in incredibly severe heat, perhaps being bombed by a variety of pyroclastics (objects, often molten, launched high into the sky by volcanic eruptions).

The only real form of protection from the latter type of eruption is to have had enough warning not to be in the area when it happens.

▼ Lava flows may be slow-flowing but they travel with molten intensity. Get well away from the locality.

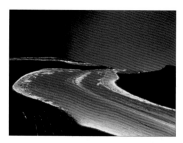

Volcanoes usually "grumble" for a long time before erupting, and science can warn of the danger. If you do find yourself there when it happens, all you can do is move directly away from the eruption as fast as possible, using far-away landmarks to help you navigate.

TSUNAMI

On 26 December 2004 an earthquake under the sea in Indonesia triggered a series of deadly waves which fanned out across the Indian Ocean and crashed on to shores – some as high as 20m/65ft – from Asia to Africa, killing over 140,000 people and leaving millions destitute. It brought to everyone's consciousness the word "tsunami", the Japanese word for tidal wave. They are not in fact caused by the tides but by earthquakes, landslides and volcanic eruptions – anything causing massive displacement of water. A tidal wave is not like an ordinary wave. It is more like a sudden increase in water level spilling across the ocean, and usually has several sequential wave fronts.

If you hear of an earthquake, a tidal wave might well be heading your way from the quake zone. Do not stay in low-lying coastal areas if this occurs. Sometimes the waters recede from the coast minutes before a tidal wave arrives. If this happens, put curiosity aside and run as fast as you can for high ground.

▲ *This tsunami sign warns of a risk. Heed the warning especially if the water suddenly recedes dramatically. Head inland and uphill.*

▲ *A tsunami can occur anywhere in an ocean that has undersea geological movement. The coastline affected might be calm or, as seen here, quite rough water.*

▲ *Before a tsunami the waters will often recede – this is the classic warning signal and the time to run for the hills, not to stroll on to the beach to pick up stranded fish.*

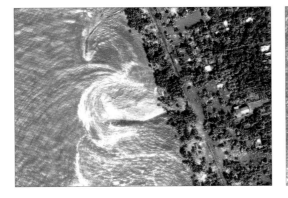

▲ *As the water surges back on to the shore a thousand tonnes of water crashes down on each metre of beach. In this whitewater zone the waves reached 10m/33ft.*

▲ *The water will continue to surge on to the land, moving much farther inshore than any normal tide, floods or storms, and demolishing almost everything in its path.*

FLASH FLOODS

It is important to know whether you are in an area that might be prone to flooding, and how high you are above typical flood levels, so that you are in a position to respond accordingly if a flood warning is issued.

If significant flooding is imminent, do not stack sandbags around the building to keep water out. Water beneath the ground may collect around the foundations and cause the entire building to "float" upwards causing structural damage. It is usually better to allow the flood water into the lower levels of the house. If you know it will flood anyway, consider deliberately flooding the basement to equalize the pressure inside and out.

• Switch off the electricity supply at the main distribution box.
• Store drinking water in clean, sealed containers since the water supply may be contaminated for some time to come.
• Disconnect any electrical appliances that cannot be moved, and decamp upstairs with any other possessions.

▼ *If you have to hang on to a tree or other fixed object in moving water, make sure you do it from the downstream side, as shown.*

▶ *If you have to, you can drive through flooded water. Work out where the shallowest water is – in this case it seems to be on the right, but it pays to check first.*

GROUP CROSSING A FLOODED RIVER

1 Find a place with anchor points (trees or rocks) and let a strong swimmer cross with two ropes. Check for any hidden dangers downstream or upstream.

2 Once across, tie a line between the two banks. The others can now haul their way across the water. A second, hand-held rope gives extra grip.

3 Equipment can be attached to the fixed rope with a karabiner and hauled across in a similar way. Make sure you keep both ends of the haul rope safely at either bank unless the river is narrow enough to throw the gear across.

4 The last member of the party can untie everything from the departure bank and be hauled across safely by the rest of the group. This is the most dangerous part, so this person should be strong and confident in the water.

▲ *Storms of any kind can cause trees or pylons to fall on to buildings, roads or cars. Avoid going out during a storm and keep an eye on vulnerable parts of your house.*

DRIVING THROUGH FLOODS

When driving through flood waters, put the car in low gear and drive very slowly. Try to avoid water splashing up into the engine area of petrol cars and affecting the ignition system. If practical, disconnect any electric cooling fan in the engine bay and remove any low-level mechanical one – this will stop the fans throwing water over the engine. Diesel vehicles are unaffected by water as long as water doesn't enter the engine through the air intake/air filter or the fuel tank through the filler or breather pipe. Be aware of these two. Remember brakes may not work well when wet.

Try to check the depth of water by having someone walk ahead tethered to a rope. A well-sealed car may begin to float in only 60cm/2ft of water – it could be very dangerous if the car starts floating away. Be certain the level is no higher than your knees or a car's wheels.

DEFENSIVE SWIMMING TECHNIQUES

If swimming in fast-moving water, maintain a defensive swimming posture with feet up and downstream (*see below*). Look ahead for obstructions. A current of 5–6.5kmh/3–4mph can pin you irrevocably to railings or fences causing almost certain drowning – be ready to swim out of the way of any such obstructions. Do not try to grab lamp posts or anything similar – you will just hurt yourself. If you're going to hit something try to fend off with your

▲ *You can get on to the roof of your house by going upstairs and pushing off some tiles from the inside – this will be much safer than going outside into the flood waters.*

feet and push around it to one side, whichever way more of the current is going. Wait for an opportunity to swim into an eddy or the safety of shallow water. Do not try to stand unless the water is under 30cm/12in deep.

If possible wear a buoyancy aid (personal flotation device). Do not enter buildings that may be damaged by flooding unless necessary. Do not approach people in trouble in the water until you have calmed them down and ensured that they won't endanger you. It is common for rescuers to be injured or even drowned by relieved victims climbing on them to get out of the water.

TACKLING THE CURRENT

▲ *You need a strong staff to give you triangular support – vital so you don't get carried away by the current.*

▲ *If you get caught in the current go feet-first and keep your head above the water with your feet and backside raised.*

▲ *You are only as secure as your weakest link so be extra vigilant if you use a human chain to pull partners across.*

STORM ACTION

Abnormal weather conditions such as hurricanes and typhoons will be forecast on the radio, television and internet. Heed any advice – in coastal areas you might need to abandon your home and move inland to higher ground. Otherwise stay at home, bring in loose objects from the garden, barricade the windows, put away valuables, and gather together emergency supplies, including water. If the storm hits, head for the basement or under the stairs, or hide under furniture. Keep listening to the forecasts.

TROPICAL STORMS

Fuelled by the ocean, hurricanes are extremely powerful winds generated by tropical storms that form in the North Atlantic Ocean and Northeast Pacific. moving up the coastline. Cyclones are formed over the South Pacific and Indian Ocean, and typhoons form over the Northwest Pacific Ocean. What they all have in common is that they can be highly destructive in a short amount of time.

Over the sea, a tropical storm can whip up huge waves and when they reach land they can cause flooding over large areas including in towns and cities.

▲ *There is little you can do in the face of a hurricane except to hide from them. Don't stay inside a building that could be destroyed by one, such as this timber-built house.*

Over land the same strong winds can flatten homes, knock over trees and even tip over cars.

Once they begin to swing inland they lose their power after a few days because there is no warm sea water to power them. Fortunately there are highly sophisticated weather monitoring systems that can identify approaching storms and the authorities can keep you informed. If you are living on high

ground and have not been instructed to flee, stay indoors. Secure anything that might blow away and board up all windows. If there is a lull in the storm be aware that you might be in the eye of the hurricane and the severity might increase again. Away from home, do not shelter in your car. It would be better to lie in a ditch, but if there is nothing suitable then consider hiding under your car.

▼ *The safest place in the wake of a tornado is underground in a tunnel or basement. Outside, get into a ditch or depression to shelter from the wind and flying debris.*

▶ *You are unlikely to be struck by lightning in a city. But in the back yard of your suburban house it is a real possibility. Go indoors at the first sound of thunder.*

TORNADO

A tornado is a funnel-shaped storm capable of tremendous destruction with wind speeds of 400kph/250mph or more. Damage paths can extend to 1.6km/1 mile wide and 80km/50 miles long. If you see a tornado, try to move out of its way at right angles to the direction it seems to be travelling. Cars, caravans and mobile homes are usually tossed around by tornadoes so head for a more solid shelter. If there is no escape, lie flat, sheltered in a ditch if possible. If you are indoors, follow the same rules as for tropical storms.

LIGHTNING

During a thunderstorm, each flash of cloud-to-ground lightning is a potential killer and although some victims are struck directly by the main lightning stroke, others are struck as the current moves in and along the ground. Lightning can be dangerous quite some way from the eye of the storm. If you can hear thunder then you are within 16km/10 miles of a storm and can be struck by lighting. It is also worth remembering that the threat of lightning continues for a much longer period than most people realise. Wait at least 30 minutes after the last thunder clap before leaving shelter.

If caught in an electrical storm, try to get inside a large building or a vehicle with a metal roof, but keep yourself away from the metal sides. If you are able to get inside a building then stay away from windows and doors and avoid contacting anything that conducts electricity, including landline telephones. If you can't get to safety, avoid being a vertical pinnacle, or being near to one. Stay low. Get away from open water. Put down objects like walking sticks or golf clubs. Stay away from small sheds or structures in open ground as they won't offer you any protection from lighting. If in a forest, find an area where the trees are small and close together.

If you are hopelessly exposed and feel a build-up of energy, tingling spine or hair standing on end, drop to the ground and curl up. Those struck by lightning do not retain the charge and are not "electrified". They can be handled immediately. Quick resuscitation is essential – for further advice, see the chapter on life-saving first aid. Cardiac arrest and irregularities, burns and nerve damage are common in cases where people are struck by lightning. Some people who seem unhurt may need attention later – check everyone for burns at the extremities and near to metal buckles or jewellery.

▲ *Lightning and trees don't mix – stay away from them. Make for low, level ground and jettison any metal objects on you.*

▲ *Get out of water fast if there is lightning. Anything wet reduces insulation. If you are trapped bend your head down and hug your knees to your chest.*

Forest fires

Recently unprecedented wildfires have caused havoc across the world. Australia battled its largest bush fire on record, while parts of California, the Amazon jungle and central Asia have also faced unusually severe blazes. Changes in the global climate with warmer, drier conditions is likely to increase the risk, timing and severity of forest fires. If travelling through dry forests or brush, do not start any kind of fire or leave optical items like glasses anywhere that could magnify the sun's rays and start a fire. If you see or hear of a fire, try to stay upwind of it and get away if you can. Search for a natural firebreak: an area without combustible material. This could be a road or a clear-cut area of woods, a boulder field or a body of water.

Do not try to outrun a forest fire if it is close, as a wall of flame can move at 32kmph/20mph, which is faster than you can run. Make for the nearest water and get into it, keeping yourself soaked and away from anything on shore that might burn. Rocks may become very hot and the water might warm up, but the water will not get hot enough to harm you unless it is a huge fire and a very shallow or stagnant stream or pond. Avoid smoke inhalation by making a mask from some clothing or similar. The fire may deprive the area

of oxygen so remain still and breathe normally to conserve it.

If you cannot get to water, you might try to clear an area around you of flammables. This will only save you in a small bushfire, not a huge forest fire where you need to run for safety. Remember also to stay outside and out of hollows and caves.

If a large forest fire approaches your built-up area, there will come a point where you have to abandon the building and flee because the enormous heat will start igniting things all around and you'll be forced to fall back. The width of a street is not enough to stop the fire reaching you in this situation. You will need

▲ *Bushfires generate a lot of smoke and people can die from smoke inhalation before the fire front reaches them. It's safer to be in a building than in a vehicle or on foot, and though a building can burn down, cleared ground around the building may survive the passage of the flame front unscathed.*

to decide when to grab your bug out bag and flee. Moving out on foot is possibly faster than by vehicle since the roads will be jammed with others with the same idea, but the fire would probably be advancing faster than you can sustain, so you must leave in good time. Ideally, the authorities will have put a retreat and evacuation plan in place for you.

ESCAPING FOREST FIRES

1 Check the smoke to see the wind direction and run away from that. The flame front can travel at 8kph/5mph.

2 Head for any natural fire break such as a stream. Stay in the water, where you should be safe from leaping flames.

3 If the fire is getting really close and scorching, lie as low as you can in the stream and stay there for safety.

Pandemics

The 1918 influenza pandemic, which ran amok from 1918 to 1920, infected an estimated one-third of the world's population and killed between 20 to 50 million people. More recently, the SARS epidemic, Covid-19, and even more lethal Ebola outbreaks have forcefully demonstrated how quickly and destructively a serious illness can devastate populations and bring normal life to a shuddering halt in a world so interconnected by modern transport. We are getting better at this, but global infectious diseases are likely to remain a part of our experience going forward.

Being in good health to start with, ensuring good nutrition with no vitamin or mineral deficiencies, and taking regular exercise is a good protection against future health threats. When a serious infectious disease is prevalent, however, this won't be enough. The first thing to consider is how to minimize your risk of infection, and that means social distancing and, wherever possible, isolation in the home. Many diseases are airborne and so owning a sensible

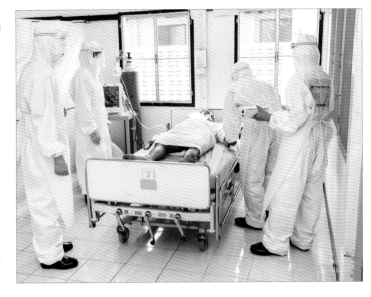

▼ *A medical threat can cause immediate food shortages that take a long time to iron out. At least these people are queueing for food, not fighting over it!*

stock of suitable face coverings and the supplies you need to maintain hygiene (anti-bacterial and anti-viral handwash, for instance) at all times will alleviate the need to join the melée of panicky shoppers when the situation does arise. Some infections, however, are waterborne and you should have the ability to boil and/or filter your drinking water.

If you are well-prepared, you should already have good stocks of

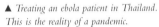

▲ *Treating an ebola patient in Thailand. This is the reality of a pandemic.*

foods that won't go off (see Survival In The Home). This means that you'll only need to go out to buy expendable items once a week. Don't deplete your home stocks. When you do have to shop, resupply the canned or dried items you have used. That way, if shopping becomes impossible, you have the basics to survive for months.

Food for long-term storage tends to be of lower nutritional value than fresh ingredients. It's easy to get enough calories but harder to ensure a healthy vitamin and mineral intake. Frozen vegetables should be stocked if possible, and items such as cereals and dairy produce that are fortified with vitamins. Keeping vitamin supplements couldn't hurt, either.

If extreme isolation becomes necessary, you may have to draw on the mental health practices we have covered earlier in the book. It's also possible that if your area becomes problematic because of pandemic-related issues, you may have to bug out (see pages 84–87).

Electricity blackouts

If a society is suddenly stripped of its electricity access dire consequences inevitably follow. Mostly due to an ongoing political crisis, Venezuela started to have electricity blackouts in January 2019 when its energy distribution infrastructure collapsed. The lack of running water, food supplies and communication capacity that plagued the country led to many deaths and considerable deprivation and suffering. Early 2021 saw the southern states of America grind to a halt with extreme cold weather storms resulting in huge areas losing power for days. It's a terrifying glimpse into the consequences of modern states being deprived of electricity for prolonged periods.

MAGNETIC FIELD REVERSAL
Many scientists believe we are overdue for a reversal of the Earth's magnetic field. The last one took place 780,000 years ago, so we only know about it because of geological studies. Some scientists believe it may be a gradual event, not so likely to cause a sudden upset of technology, wildlife and climate. The latest data appears to show that the Earth's molten magnetic core is not the simple dipole magnet that scientists assumed, but a chaotic jumble of different forces held in a delicate balance that (fairly) irregularly flips. If a more rapid reversal took place it would likely cause a significant interruption of technology including electricity generation and distribution, communications and logistics. It's not just a matter of the compass needle flipping round.

Another effect would be that animals using the Earth's magnetic field for navigation – this includes

▶ The smoke trail after a meteorite exploded over Chelyabinsk, Russian Federation. The devastation from this massive airburst was considerable and it was a miracle no one was killed.

birds, some fish and amphibians – might become lost and disorientated during migrations. It is difficult to predict the knock-on effect this might have on all life. Furthermore, if the magnetic field gets weaker (as is predicted) and stays that way for a long time, the Earth will be less protected from the powerful electromagnetic radiation that exists in interplanetary space. This would mean that everything could be exposed to more radiation, which could also harm delicate electronics and power supplies on Earth and in the long term could increase the incidence of diseases like cancer.

▲ Families gather on the streets of Caracas to collect water from a central point. Water shortages were caused by a six-day power cut across Venezuela in March 2019.

METEOROID STRIKE
Most of us are aware that large extraterrestrial objects striking the Earth has potential for a catastrophic number of deaths. The dinosaurs were wiped out by just such an event. What fewer people realise is how many lucky escapes we have. The Tunguska event of 1908 happened over a very sparsely populated area of Siberia, but the explosion of the meteoroid at an altitude of several

miles still flattened around eighty million trees. It's easy to see what would have happened to a town or city and its population, had there been one in the area. More recently, the Chelyabinsk disaster of 2013 did result in thousands of injuries and a great deal of property damage. The 20m/66ft Chelyabinsk meteor also exploded high above the Earth because of a shallow angle of entry, delivering destructive energy estimated to be 30 times that of the Hiroshima atom bomb. Most of the injuries were caused by flying glass, but with a slightly steeper entry angle things could have turned out very differently. The most frightening thing about this event is that despite 21st-century technology, the authorities had no idea it was coming.

POWER SUPPLY BACK-UP

Despite the robust technology of the 21st century, we all experience power cuts now and again. Inconvenient though these are, we almost always have the supply restored before the food goes bad in the freezer or the battery runs out on the laptop computer. In a disaster scenario, the power won't come back on in that kind of timescale. Therefore, it would be wise to prepare to keep essential utilities working for at least a week. A month would be better. A small generator would be adequate to keep the fridge and freezer working and perhaps charge the batteries in small essential equipment. But it would be better still if you could keep your household running reasonably normally. Since this would require an enormous generator, a better solution would be solar panels recharging a battery bank large enough to power the house through the night. Many homes have solar, but most of them feed the power to the supply grid rather than storing it in batteries. However, you can invest in a UPS (Uninterruptable Power Supply), which switches seamlessly from mains to battery power in an outage event. The solar panels recharge the batteries. With this method, your security systems like burglar alarm, motion sensors, and night vision cameras are still up – even your wi-fi and connectivity if the internet is working. Hint – in a prolonged power cut, it probably won't be. See Telecommunications.

NUCLEAR DETONATION

Governments strive to maintain agreements that will prevent a nuclear war from ever taking place, but a nuclear attack could still happen if weapons fall into the wrong hands, or there could be an accidental detonation. The main thing to consider is that a catastrophe on this scale cannot be ameliorated by the authorities and that all the trappings of civilization are going to be down for a considerable period of time, partly because of the widespread damage to buildings and infrastructure by the explosion, and also because the electromagnetic pulse from such a blast will fry every piece of electronics within range. Nothing we are accustomed to in modern life will function for a very long time.

ELECTROMAGNETIC PULSE

An Electromagnetic Pulse or EMP is a very short, very powerful burst of energy which can be a natural phenomenon or man-made. Short-range EMP generators can be used as weapons to damage equipment, but the massive EMP released by nuclear events or explosions can wipe out an entire electricity supply grid and potentially destroy any devices that are connected and switched on.

SOLAR FLARE – THE CARRINGTON EFFECT

Solar flares are a constant feature of our sun, that come and go in cycles of severity, but in some instances, huge ones can generate an enormous geomagnetic storm. Such coronal mass ejections as they are called

TELECOMMUNICATIONS

In the event of a major catastrophe, there's a good chance that telecommunications will be one of the early casualties. Even if the internet, landlines and cellphone signal aren't taken out immediately, there's a good chance they will be if a power outage persists for more than a few hours. Most cellphone towers, in particular, have a UPS sufficient to keep them online for 2–4 hours. After that, no calls or SMS, and the internet will only reach your phone if your wi-fi router still has power. If the landline is still in service, you'll need mains power to your base station unless you own a fixed phone that doesn't require a power cord.

In recent long-term outages in the Western world, most of the telecoms have been down pretty quickly, making it troublesome to call for help and hard to keep in touch with your neighbours for security or your loved ones for emotional support. Cheap two-way radio handsets from any toy store can be a lifesaver in this situation. If someone needs to go out for supplies, they can take a handset. If you hear a disturbance, you can call the neighbours on the radio. Other options, which may require a licence, are Family Radio Service in the US, CB radio, and HAM radio. Whichever one you use, any HAM radio enthusiasts in range will hear transmissions from all of them, which means that they can act as a hub for different users and even contact the emergency services for you by radio.

(sometimes named Carrington Events after the British astronomer Richard Carrington) are accompanied by solar EMP's that have already been observed knocking out the power grid of developed countries. Such events are unpredictable, subject to the solar cycle, and could happen anywhere at any time.

LIFE-SAVING FIRST AID

Understanding first aid, and how to apply it, is crucial in serious
emergencies. If you know the basic techniques you can sustain a victim
of an accident or sudden emergency until professional help arrives on
the scene. Even at home or on a crowded street, the support you give
can mean the difference between life and death. If you find yourself
stranded in a remote or dangerous environment, perhaps when travelling
or under sudden attack, you'll be much farther away from paramedics,
so you really need to know what to do.

Assembling a first-aid kit

Our daily activities are usually relatively low-risk; most people live and work in a place with good road access so that an ambulance could reach them without too much delay, so a well-stocked first-aid kit and the knowledge to use it will be as much as they need. A casualty will certainly feel much calmer if you show that you can dress and bandage an injury professionally. However, nothing in a first-aid kit is as important as you and your ability to act sensibly and think on your feet. Communication is

▼ *Do a detailed check through your first-aid kit after each trip and replace anything that has been used or has deteriorated.*

also very important, so make the best use of telephones, neighbours or passers-by if you are able to.

BASIC KIT

Make sure that all the items in the kit are well marked and that the kit is kept dry and clean. If necessary, this may mean stowing the container in a waterproof case or bag.

For cuts and grazes, include a good selection of adhesive dressings, both waterproof and fabric-backed. Non-adhesive dressings should be sealed in protective wrappings. Take plenty of sterile gauze pads, the best dressing to stop bleeding from a small wound and

STANDARD KIT

- Surgical gloves
- Wound dressings (2.5–15cm/ 1–6in)
- Antiseptic wipes
- Assorted adhesive plasters
- Scissors
- Triangular bandages
- Tweezers
- Crêpe bandages
- Sterile scalpel blades
- Moleskin
- Sterile needles
- Sterile gauze pads
- Thermometer
- Cotton wool (balls)
- Safety pins
- Lint
- Roll of adhesive tape
- Sterilized strips (used to close wounds)
- Water purification tablets
- Portable splint
- Face mask for mouth-to-mouth resuscitation

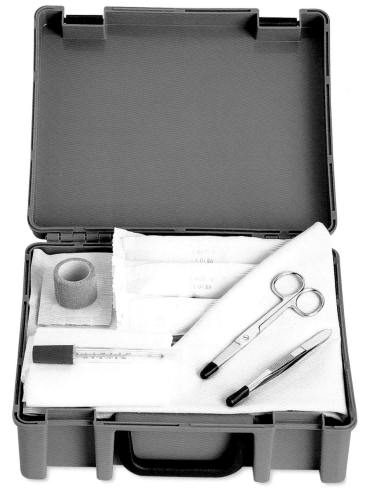

to dress most small to medium-sized wounds, secured with roller bandages. Adhesive tape is an alternative, but some people are allergic to this: try to check before using it. Cotton wool (balls) can be carried to clean the skin around a wound but not to dress an open wound, as the fluff will stick to it.

Scissors in the kit should be sharp, but should have one rounded side to allow the safe cutting of dressings and clothing (for example when treating burns or scalds) without the risk of cutting the skin.

Always carry a notebook and pen in your first-aid kit. In case of serious illness or injury this will allow you to record regular observations of the victim until they can be attended to by a medical practitioner.

Know where the first-aid kit is kept at work, at home and in the car, so that wherever you are when an emergency occurs, a casualty can be made comfortable until help arrives.

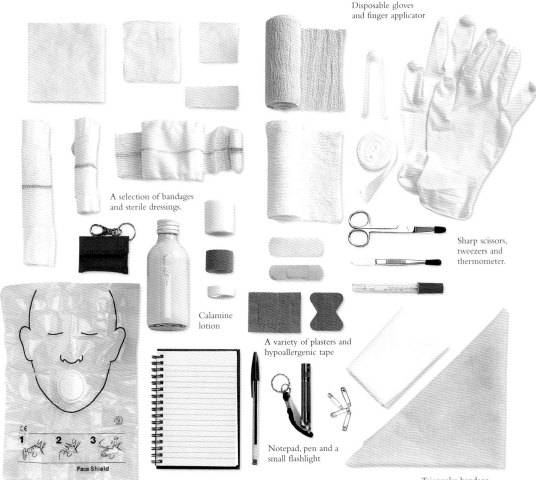

Disposable gloves
and finger applicator

A selection of bandages
and sterile dressings.

Sharp scissors,
tweezers and
thermometer.

Calamine
lotion

A variety of plasters and
hypoallergenic tape

Face Shield

Notepad, pen and a
small flashlight

Triangular bandage

▲ *A standard first-aid kit is equipped to support essential life-saving procedures and deal with a range of common injuries; it does not include any drugs or medicines.*

WHEN TRAVELLING

If you are planning a trip you may incur specific risks, either of illness or accident, which you should make yourself aware of and prepare for. The standard first-aid kit is designed to facilitate basic life-saving procedures and deal with common injuries, and you may need to augment its contents. Consider what risks you could encounter and make sure your kit will cover these. If you need to carry more items than those included in the standard kit, add only those that your doctor has recommended and that you

have been trained how to use, to avoid adding unnecessary weight.

If you are going on a long trip in the developing world, you may wish to add a sterile needle kit and an emergency dental kit, in case you have to seek the help of qualified practitioners who are coping with a shortage of medical equipment.

In hot countries, there may be more illnesses and infections than accidents to be dealt with, and this should be reflected in the contents of the kit and any training undertaken.

AT WORK

The qualified first aider at work should be in charge of the office first-aid kit. All workers are advised to know where the kit is and how to use it.

DRUGS AND MEDICINES

Any drugs or medicines you add to your kit will be a matter of discussion between you and your doctor, but you will need at least the following:
• Painkillers, both medium and strong
• Treatment for constipation
• Antiseptic cream and powder
• Calamine lotion to soothe sunburn and rashes
• Motion sickness remedies
• Insect repellent
• Eye wash or eye drops or ointment
• Antihistamines
• Rehydration solutions

Assessing an injured person

First aid help can cover an extremely varied range of scenarios – from simple reassurance after a small accident to dealing with a life-threatening emergency. A speedy response is crucial. Emergency workers refer to the first hour after an accident as the golden hour: the more help given within this hour, the better the outcome for the patient. If an accident happens and somebody is badly wounded or unconscious, they will not be able to describe their injuries to you, and you will have to ascertain what help is needed by assessing what you see and hear. The DRABC Code (below) leads you through the initial step-by-step assessment.

WHAT TO DO IN AN EMERGENCY

First, STAY CALM. Secondly, ASSESS THE SITUATION promptly. Now carry out the "DRABC" sequence, as follows:

1 DANGER
Your assessment should have alerted you to any potential hazards. Now you should:
- Keep yourself out of any danger.
- Keep passers-by out of danger.
- Make safe any hazards, if you can do so without endangering yourself or others. Only move the casualty away from danger in extreme circumstances.

2 RESPONSE
Try to establish the responsiveness level.
- If the casualty appears unconscious or semi-conscious, speak loudly to them – as in "Can you hear me?".
- If this fails to get a response, tap them firmly on the shoulders (or elsewhere if they have a shoulder injury).

THE DRABC CODE
Remembering and acting on these can save lives:

D for DANGER
R for RESPONSE
A for AIRWAY
B for BREATHING
C for CIRCULATION

THE GOALS OF FIRST AID
- To summon urgent medical help when necessary.
- To keep the casualty alive. The ABC of life support – Airway, Breathing and Circulation – constitutes the absolute top priority of first aid.
- To stop the casualty getting worse.
- To promote their recovery.
- To provide reassurance and comfort to the casualty.

▼ *Always make your initial assessment of a casualty in the position in which you found them.*

3 AIRWAY
Now determine whether the airway (the passage from the mouth to the lungs) is clear enough to allow proper breathing.
- Check the mouth and remove any visible obvious obstructions, such as food, that are at the front of the mouth only.
- Tilt the casualty's head back gently to prevent the tongue from falling back and blocking the airway. Place a hand on the forehead/top of head and two fingers under the jaw. Tilt back gently until a natural stop is reached.

▲ *Never jump in the water when dealing with a potential drowning. Hand the person something to hold on to. If nothing is available, lie down and extend your arms so that they can haul themselves up to the safety of the bank.*

◀ *Always try to get help from passers-by. Ideally, ask someone to call the emergency services while you stay with the casualty; keep them warm until trained aid arrives.*

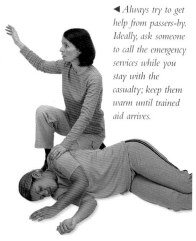

▶ *Tilt the head using a hand on the forehead/top of head and two fingers under the jaw. This casualty was found on his back. Avoid moving a casualty on to their back unless you need to start resuscitation.*

4 BREATHING

Is the casualty breathing?

- LOOK to see if the chest is moving.
- LISTEN for breathing sounds – put your ear against their mouth.
- FEEL for expired air by placing your cheek or ear close to their face.
- CHECK for breathing for about 10 seconds. If these checks are negative... CALL FOR AN AMBULANCE; ideally get someone else to do so. Make sure you tell the emergency services that the person is not breathing.
- Without delay, start CPR (cardio-pulmonary resuscitation) with chest compressions alone, or if trained and willing to do so, with rescue breaths as well as chest compressions. The emergency dispatcher may be able to tell you if there is a public access defibrillator nearby. If so, or if you know of one's location, send someone to get it if you can. If you are alone, do not stop CPR in order to fetch it yourself.

5 CIRCULATION

Look for signs of a working circulation.

- If you have established that the person is breathing, check for signs of severe bleeding by looking systematically down the body, on both sides.
- Treat severe bleeding promptly by compressing with a dressing or clothing or gloved hand. CALL FOR AN AMBULANCE, and monitor for shock.
- If there is no severe bleeding, then check for other injuries or illnesses.

GETTING HELP

If the casualty is inside a building and other people are present, ask someone to stand outside the building in order to guide the emergency services.

DON'T MOVE THEM!

There are good reasons for leaving a casualty in place until more skilled personnel arrive. Injuries to the spine, especially to the neck, are possible after accidents and falls, and further movement can cause serious damage to

▼ *Look, listen and feel for any signs of normal breathing, such as the chest moving up and down.*

▼ *If there are no signs of breathing, start CPR: chest compressions only or chest compressions with rescue breaths if you are trained to give them.*

INFORMATION FOR THE EMERGENCY SERVICES

- Your location (ideally the postal or zip code, but a landmark will do if you know no more) and the phone number you are calling from.
- What the problem is and what time it happened.

This is sufficient for the emergency operator to send an ambulance if required. While waiting, other information that may be helpful may include:

- Whether the casualty is conscious and breathing, and if they have any chest pain.
- The patient's age, sex and any medical history you know.
- If it is relevant, how many casualties there are, and their sex and approximate age.
- Any hazards, such as ice on the road or hazardous substances.

The operator may ask further questions and is trained to give instructions over the phone for potentially life-saving procedures.

VITAL NUMBERS

Some national emergency services numbers:

- UK: 999
- US: 911
- Australia: 000 On cellphones, use these numbers or 112 (but check with your network).

the spinal cord. You may have to use some movement to deal with an injury, but the golden rule after an accident is not to move an injured person unless they are in danger, need to be resuscitated, or are unconscious and should be put into the recovery position. If moving a casualty is unavoidable, you must be extremely careful with their neck.

▼ *If someone falls from a height, keep them warm and do not move them – unless it is necessary for resuscitation.*

Rescue and resuscitation

Chest compressions are also known as cardiac compressions, or as cardiac/chest/heart massage. These compressions form part of the CIRCULATION stage of DRABC. If you are faced with a casualty who is not responding and not breathing properly, you must immediately start to give compressions to initiate cardiopulmonary resuscitation (CPR).

You do not need to give mouth-to-mouth respiration unless you are trained and willing to do so: CPR using chest compressions alone greatly increases the survival rate after cardiac arrest.

For chest compressions to be effective, the casualty should be lying flat on their back on a firm surface such as the floor – or the ground if they are outside. Although it is a good idea to practise finding the CPR compression site before you need to act in an emergency, never carry out practice compressions on conscious volunteers, as you may cause harm. Always use a first aid dummy.

WARNING
In general, do not check for a pulse when assessing a person unless you are highly trained and can check it rapidly, without wasting vital seconds. It is not easy to find a pulse, even for trained people. People can die when first-aiders mistakenly feel a non-existent pulse, and fail to resuscitate. Instead of checking for a pulse, check the casualty's responsiveness and whether they are breathing normally. This should take no more than a few seconds. Remember, occasional gasps are not effective breathing.

DEFIBRILLATORS
An automatic external defibrillator (AED) is a device that applies an electric shock to the chest in order to re-start the heart, so buying valuable time for a victim of cardiac arrest. The device analyses the heart rhythm and delivers a shock where necessary. AEDs may be life-saving, particularly if the emergency services take more than five minutes to arrive. Portable versions of these life-saving machines are now frequently available in public locations such as shopping malls, sports and fitness facilities, education institutions, public buildings, and public parks, as well as in many workplaces. The devices are designed for use by untrained people and are very simple to use. Emergency operators may know the location of your nearest AED and how to access it, and can give instructions on using it.

IMPROVING SURVIVAL
Because early initiation of chest compressions vastly improves survival rates, experts now recommend that bystanders should perform compression-only CPR in cases of adult cardiac arrest, and attempt rescue breaths ("kiss of life") as well only if trained and willing to do so. The use of chest compressions alone gives survival rates at least similar to those of traditional CPR with compressions plus artificial ventilation.

HOW TO FIND THE COMPRESSION SITE

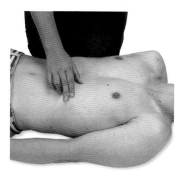

1 Kneel beside the casualty and run the fingers of your hand nearest the waist along the lower ribs until they meet the breastbone at the centre of the ribcage.

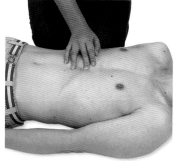

2 Keeping your middle finger at this notch, place the index finger of the same hand over the lower end of the breastbone.

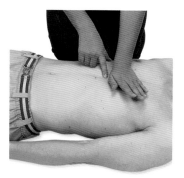

3 Place the heel of the other hand on the breastbone, and slide it down to lie beside the index finger already there. The heel of your hand is now on the compression site.

HOW TO GIVE CARDIAC MASSAGE

1 Kneel down at right angles to the casualty, so that you are positioned roughly halfway between their shoulders and waist.

2 Locate the compression site, and place the heel of one hand over this area. Place the heel of the other hand on top with both sets of fingers interlaced. The heels of your hands are going to do the work; your fingers should not touch the chest. Keep your elbows locked and arms straight all the time.

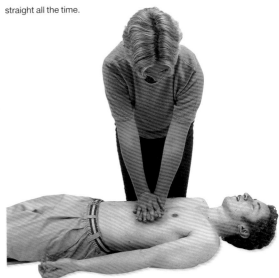

3 Place your shoulders directly over your hands so you are leaning over the casualty. This will concentrate pressure at the compression site. Compress the chest wall down by about 5–6cm (2–2½in). Release the pressure without taking your hands off the chest or bending your elbows.

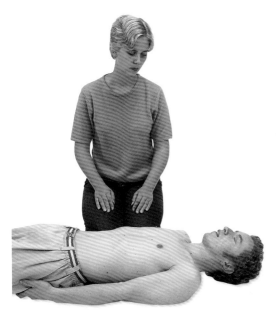

4 Using your body weight as well as your arms, push down on the chest at a rate of 100–120 compressions per minute – about twice per second. A helpful way to get the rate right is to pace your compressions to the imagined soundtrack of the Bee Gee's "Staying Alive", or Queen's "Another One Bites the Dust". Keep your hands on the chest and release the pressure in between pushes.

5 Continue giving compressions until help arrives. If there is more than one bystander, take turns if you can, but keep the compressions going with minimal interruption.

WARNING

Do not stop compressions because you are worried about hurting the casualty, for instance by cracking a rib. Once the heart has stopped the person will die without your help – they are better off alive and with a broken rib.

Dealing with head injuries

Serious head injury is a medical emergency, particularly if the casualty loses consciousness. The first-aider should protect the casualty's airway, start resuscitation if necessary and alert the emergency services without delay. An obvious cut or bump on the scalp may lead to a suspicion of head injury, but serious internal injury is often not evident from external signs. It is worth remembering also that very young and very old people are especially susceptible to developing delayed reactions to relatively minor head injuries – so may need checking out.

Head injuries are potentially serious because they can damage the brain and surrounding blood vessels. Although the bony skull protects the brain, it also provides an enclosed space in which the brain can be easily shaken and damaged, and where there is little room for any swelling or bleeding following injury.

The main causes of head injuries are road traffic accidents, sporting and recreational activities, falls and assaults.

▼ *A sudden, crushing headache should always be investigated, particularly if it comes on at some point after a blow to the head.*

TYPES OF HEAD INJURY

There are five main types of head injury, and casualties may have several symptoms simultaneously:

CUTS

Large cuts to the scalp look alarming, and bleed profusely, but are only likely to be serious if caused by a major blow. A large blow may cause brain damage.

CONCUSSION

This is a head injury that temporarily affects brain function. Symptoms may include loss of consciousness, confusion, dizziness, visual disturbances, nausea and vomiting, short-term memory loss, headache and behaviour or personality changes. They may arise immediately following injury nor not for some days or even weeks.

CONTUSION

Bruising, or contusion, may occur to the brain after an injury, and this causes swelling of the brain tissue. This may lead to prolonged periods of unconsciousness following a serious accident, and possibly much longer

SIGNS AND SYMPTOMS OF SERIOUS HEAD INJURY

- Deep cuts or tears to the scalp, or goose egg swelling over the scalp.
- Nausea and/or vomiting.
- Severe headache.
- Drowsiness or difficulty being roused.
- Unequal sized pupils, or pupils that do not respond to light.
- Visual disturbance.
- Blood or fluid flowing from ears, nose, eyes and/or mouth.
- Paralysis, numbness or loss of function over one half of the body.
- Problems with balance.
- Behaving as though drunk.
- Fits, confusion or unconsciousness.

▼ *A "contracoup" injury is one in which the bruising is on the opposite side to the site of the injury.*

CONTRA-COUP INJURY

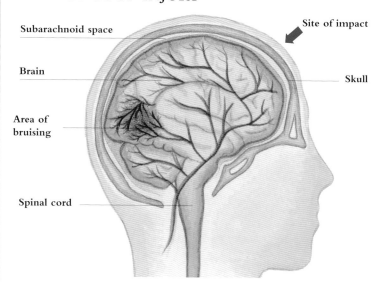

Subarachnoid space

Site of impact

Brain

Skull

Area of bruising

Spinal cord

POSSIBLE SITE OF BRAIN INJURY FOLLOWING BLOW TO BACK OF HEAD

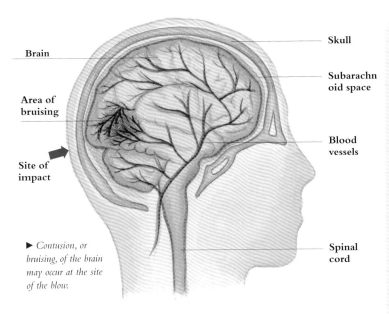

Brain

Area of bruising

Site of impact

Skull

Subarachnoid space

Blood vessels

Spinal cord

▶ *Contusion, or bruising, of the brain may occur at the site of the blow.*

periods of amnesia after regaining consciousness.

In addition there may be signs of brain injury in other parts of the body, such as paralysis, numbness or changes in breathing. The bruising may be directly at the site of the injury, or it may be on the opposite side of the skull as the brain bounces away – this is called a contra-coup brain injury.

HAEMORRHAGE

Bleeding within the skull, or intracranial haemorrhage, is a common consequence of a major head injury. The tough sheath (dura mater) attached to the inside of the skull is well supplied with blood vessels. These may be damaged and cause bleeding; sometimes the effects are delayed for several weeks after the injury has occurred.

COMPRESSION

The skull is an enclosed space, and if there is any swelling or bleeding within it, a point is reached when there is no more room for expansion. Compression of the brain can lead to quite severe

SIGNS AND SYMPTOMS OF RISING PRESSURE WITHIN THE SKULL

• Intense headache, worse when lying flat and/or with physical exertion.
• Vomiting.
• Unequal or dilated pupils.
• Weakness on one side of the body.
• Noisy, irregular breathing.
• Irritable or aggressive breathing.

damage and a wide range of symptoms (see box above). In certain extreme cases, it can cause brain tissue to squeeze out of the base of the skull – a condition known as coning. This is fatal so it is absolutely vital that any rise in pressure within the skull is recognized before this happens.

Even after seemingly minor head injuries, always be very vigilant for signs of increased cerebral pressure and get help promptly if you spot any.

HEAD INJURY FIRST AID

Breathing in vomit while unconscious after a head injury may be fatal. The first priority is to protect the victim's airway by tilting back the jaw. Always assume that they may have spinal injuries and protect their neck while trying to keep their airway open. If they are not breathing, start resuscitation.

Carefully apply direct pressure to any scalp wounds that are bleeding.

Watch for vomiting.

If they are conscious, lay them on the floor with head and shoulders slightly raised. If unconscious, place them in the recovery position while protecting their neck.

Call the emergency services.

Check to see how alert they are. Reassure them if they are alert.

Continue to watch their breathing, circulation and level of consciousness until help arrives and be prepared to resuscitate if necessary. Even if they regain consciousness, insist that they go to hospital to be checked out.

Managing crush injuries

A casualty who has suffered a crush injury requires the urgent attention of paramedics, and immediate ambulance transfer to hospital. Crush injuries can occur in road accidents, from falling heavy furniture in buildings that suffer structural damage, and in industrial and agricultural accidents when someone is crushed by heavy machinery. The crush injury may result in serious complications, so it is essential to call the emergency services as quickly as possible, and to control any external bleeding until help arrives.

In all cases involving trapped casualties or crush injuries, call the emergency services immediately. As well as paramedics, the fire service may be needed to release the casualty. Only attempt to do so yourself if you can do so safely.

CRUSHED HANDS, FINGERS, FEET AND TOES

If these are caught in machinery or tricky to release, leave this to the professionals. If the crushed part has already been released:
- Deal with any bleeding, and apply a sterile dressing.
- Treat as for fractures, with padding, immobilization and elevation.

CRUSHED LIMBS

The offending object may be just bulky enough to cut off the blood supply, or a hard impact or very heavy object may have caused fractures and severe tissue damage.

If left for too long, toxins, waste products and blood clots can develop in crushed limbs. When released, these may lead to fatal kidney and heart failure. However, this usually takes well over 30 minutes to occur, by

▶ *Road accidents are a major cause of crush injuries. Such accidents also have great potential for further disaster. Never step into a dangerous environment or try to release anyone if you are risking your own safety or could cause them further harm.*

which time emergency helpers will hopefully be in control. Where a crushed limb has been released, treat it as a fracture.

CRUSHED ABDOMEN AND PELVIS

Any crushing or blunt impact to the abdomen can cause severe internal bleeding and damage. The casualty may show no outward signs at first, so the accident history could be your only clue to a potentially severe condition.

The ideal first-aid position here is the "shock" position, with legs raised – unless this might worsen damage, in which case keep them still. If they need to vomit, you may need to turn them on their side. Do not sit them up. Treat a crushed pelvis as a fracture, and get help very quickly.

CRUSHED CHEST

A heavy weight on the chest can cause a casualty's breathing to stop. Check that nothing under the object is penetrating the chest and then carefully lift the object off, if you can. If breathing has stopped, start chest compressions. Conscious casualties may find it easier to breathe sitting up, but keeping them in their current position until help arrives will often prevent further damage.

MANAGING CRUSH INJURIES

- Make any threatening structures/objects safe/stable, but only if this will not endanger yourself or the casualty.
- Check the casualty's ABC (assessing the victim, breathing and circulation) and contact the emergency services.
- Release the victim if possible, but do not endanger yourself or further endanger the casualty. If the crushing force has been in place for some time, be prepared for the casualty's condition to deteriorate rapidly: keep monitoring ABC and start resuscitation if necessary.
- Treat any injuries in order of their importance and severity. If injuries involve the head or neck, make sure that these are kept still (to avoid worsening any possible spinal injury). Treat any bleeding or fractures.
- Treat for shock, but only raise the legs if you are pretty certain there are no leg fractures.
- Keep the casualty warm, still and as comfortable as possible. Continue to monitor them until help arrives.

Controlling severe bleeding

Stemming blood flow from a large wound is a life-saving procedure. The main method used combines pressure and elevation. Apply direct pressure to the site of the blood loss with your hand or the casualty's hand, unless the wound contains foreign matter such as glass. In this case, squeeze the edges of the wound together. Elevating the wounded area also helps to stem blood loss – even if a limb is fractured, your priority is to stop the bleeding, especially if it is heavy, and then worry about the fracture. However, try to handle fractured limbs gently.

Injury to an artery can lead to a life-threatening loss of blood in a very short time. Stemming the blood flow may save the casualty's life and is your main priority as a first-aider (once you have dealt with the casualty's ABC, that is).

With more superficial wounds, bleeding may sometimes seem profuse without, in fact, being too dangerous. Head wounds are a good case in point here. The scalp has a very rich blood supply, so head wounds often bleed profusely, even if they are quite superficial. Do not, however, automatically go to the other extreme and assume that it is not serious. Also, always try to assess any underlying damage – especially important with head wounds.

STEMMING BLOOD FLOW

The most effective method is applying direct pressure to the wound and, where possible, keeping the body part elevated – gravity naturally lessens the flow. If an object is embedded in the wound, compress the edges on either side of the object. Stemming blood flow by applying pressure to the main arteries supplying the bleeding site is not advised for the average first-aider – this can be tricky.

Bleeding may be copious in a head injury, and you may be hampered by the person's hair. Apply a dressing larger than the wound, bandage it in place and get medical help rapidly. If a limb is bleeding heavily, elevate it to reduce the blood flow to the area. If the wound is on a leg, lift both legs to maximize blood flow to the casualty's vital organs, especially their brain.

Even a fractured limb should be elevated if it is bleeding very profusely.

AVOID TOURNIQUETS

These should never be used to control serious bleeding except by fully trained medical professionals, and only by them as an absolute last resort. The scenario in which use of a tourniquet is most likely to occur is when a limb has been partially or wholly severed, when it has very little chance of survival anyway.

TYPES OF BLEEDING

From arteries
- Blood spurts rhythmically with the beat of the heart.
- Blood is bright red.
- Blood loss is rapid and quickly leads to shock.

From veins
- Blood is darker red with a bluish hue.
- Blood oozes steadily.
- Blood loss is slower but can eventually cause shock.

DRESSING A WOUND WITH AN EMBEDDED OBJECT

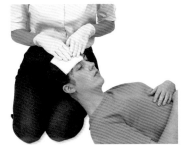

1 If the casualty is unconscious, follow DRABC before dealing with the wound – if the person is not breathing institute chest compressions without delay. Try to find the source of the bleeding – remember that there may be more than one site. If the casualty is conscious, ask them to tell you all they can about what happened, to help your assessment.

2 To control bleeding, place firm pressure directly over the wound using a clean pad (a sterile first-aid dressing or a towel, sanitary towel, tea towel or T-shirt). Use gentle pressure if you suspect a fracture. Getting the casualty to lie down with head and shoulders raised (and supported) helps to reduce pressure within the head.

3 Secure the dressing with a roller bandage or equivalent. If the casualty's general condition seems good sitting them up may reduce bleeding. Make sure that the dressing covers the whole wound. If blood starts oozing through the dressing, don't take the original dressing off but place another one on top.

Internal bleeding

It is vital that the first-aider is able to recognize the signs of internal bleeding and take appropriate action. Internal bleeding can be caused by stabbing or shooting, which also cause external bleeding, or by a fall, a crush injury, a punch or kick, a fractured bone or an ulcer, which may not. The signs include cold and clammy, pale skin, weakness, thirst, and blood coming from an orifice. Internal bleeding is a medical emergency and if you suspect it you should call the emergency services at once.

Unlike external bleeding, internal bleeding is a difficult condition to assess. It may be unclear what is happening until the problem is at a late stage, when the casualty has already bled a great deal and is going into shock. Detecting internal bleeding early on, and calling an ambulance, is by far the most helpful action you can perform under these circumstances.

CAUSES OF INTERNAL BLEEDING

Stabbing and shooting are obvious causes of internal bleeding, and the size of an external wound is often no indicator of the extent of the internal

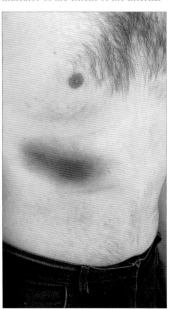

◀ *Bruising on the skin, especially if it is over the abdomen or chest, may indicate internal bleeding. Call the emergency services the minute you suspect internal bleeding. The casualty is in need of urgent medical attention. It is important not to let them eat or drink anything until they have been seen.*

SIGNS AND SYMPTOMS OF INTERNAL BLEEDING

- If someone shows signs of shock. This is indicated by: cold, clammy, pale skin; loss of consciousness on sitting or standing up; thirst and general weakness; a fast. weak pulse.
- If the victim coughs up blood or vomits blood or anything that looks like blood (bits of gritty brown vomit that look like coffee grounds are a classic sign of a bleeding duodenal ulcer).
- If they have passed blood from their rectum (back passage), especially black tar-like stools that smell strongly. This is likely to be due to a bleeding ulcer in the stomach or duodenum .
- If they have been in an accident where they fell from a height, or stopped suddenly, as in a car accident, or fell off a bicycle on to the handle bars.

- If there is profuse bleeding from the vagina with no obvious cause.
- If the casualty has bruising, tenderness and or swelling, especially if it is over the abdominal area. The kidney, spleen and liver may bleed after an accident. There may be blood in the urine, abdominal pain, and the abdomen may be swollen.
- If a woman is in the early stages of pregnancy, particularly between 6 and 8 weeks. A pregnancy in the Fallopian tube (known as an ectopic pregnancy) may cause profuse internal bleeding that is life-threatening. The woman may have warning pains low in her abdomen, but not invariably.
- If there is blood coming from the nose, ear or mouth after a head injury. This may be due to a fracture of the skull.

damage. Internal blood vessels and organs can tear and rupture without any obvious external damage.

An injury caused by an object that is not sharp enough to penetrate the skin is called "blunt trauma". This may be due to any number of causes – from a fall, a car accident or crush injury to direct punches or kicks. A warning sign of possible internal damage would be bruising on the skin, especially if it is over the abdomen or chest.

Another common cause of internal bleeding is fractured bones, especially the femur and pelvis, which quickly lead to serious blood loss. Conditions such as duodenal and gastric ulcers

may lead to profuse internal bleeding. People with blood-clotting abnormalities such as haemophilia, or who are on anti-clotting treatment such as warfarin, may bleed heavily after relatively minor injuries. Many diseases affecting the liver may adversely affect the blood's ability to clot, and may also cause varices, which are like internal varicose veins – these can bleed catastrophically.

WARNING
Signs of internal bleeding may not appear for some time after the incident that caused it, and it may be after considerable blood is lost from the circulation. This is why, if there is any risk that an accident or condition could cause internal bleeding, the casualty should be checked over promptly by a medical professional.

Bleeding from orifices

Bleeding can occur from the mouth, nose, ear, urethra, rectum or vagina (though menstrual bleeding is normal, obviously). These may require first aid to staunch the flow if possible, and you should also check for signs of shock. Bear in mind that dealing with another person's body fluids puts you and them at risk of infection, so use gloves, if they are available. If you do not have gloves, wash your hands well both before and afterwards. Bleeding from orifices with no obvious cause may indicate internal bleeding, which requires urgent medical attention.

VAGINAL BLEEDING

There can be many reasons for non-menstrual vaginal bleeding, including pregnancy problems and sexual assault. Bleeding in early pregnancy is a warning that miscarriage may be imminent or might already have occurred, and the bleeding can be very heavy, including clots that look like lumps of liver. When the bleeding is this heavy, you must get medical aid urgently.

In cases of sexual assault, the casualty is likely to be very distressed, so use great tact and care. Ideally, the casualty should not get undressed or wash until seen by the police, to aid collection of forensic evidence. Your priorities are to staunch the flow, reassure the victim and contact the emergency services.

RECTAL BLEEDING

Bleeding from the rectum can be divided into two types. Bright red blood is usually due to problems lower down in the gut, most commonly piles or a small tear after passing a difficult motion, although there may be more sinister causes. Dark, sticky, black motions indicate old blood from higher up in the gut. It is the dark blood that requires the most urgent action, as it signifies heavy bleeding that could be life-threatening.

VOMITING BLOOD

Bleeding from the stomach and upper digestive system may be bright red or resemble coffee grounds (it may also come from a swallowed nosebleed). The casualty may appear in shock, or seem almost normal. All vomiting of blood should be treated as serious. Sit the casualty down, or if pale or shocked lie them on their side, and seek urgent medical help.

COUGHING UP BLOOD

This usually appears as small spots mixed in sputum, and causes include lung disease and lung damage. Sit the casualty up, supported and quiet. If their breathing is distressed, or their history suggests lung damage, get help fast. Anyone who coughs up blood must be seen by a medical professional.

BLEEDING FROM THE MOUTH

This may arise from biting the inside of the mouth, or after a tooth has fallen out or been extracted. It can occur after violent impact, along with possible concussion or jaw fracture. The main concern should be keeping the airway clear of blood, especially if the person is unconscious.

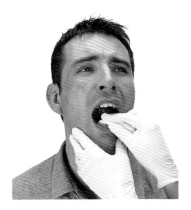

◄ *If there is bleeding from the mouth, place a wad of sterile gauze in the mouth and ask the casualty to bite down on it to stem the flow of blood. Wear gloves to protect yourself from te risk of infection.*

▲ *If there is bleeding from the ear, place a sterile pad or clean towel over the ear and tilt the head to drain out the blood. Call a doctor immediately.*

BLEEDING FROM THE NOSE

Nosebleeds usually start at the lower end of the nose, although in older people or those with very high blood pressure, they may come from the back of the nose and be harder to stop. Nosebleeds often occur during or after a cold when the lining is inflamed. Other causes are a direct impact (which may also have caused concussion or head or facial fractures), violent nose-blowing and nose-picking. Watery blood or clear fluid from the nose may arise from a fracture at the base of the skull.

BLEEDING FROM THE EAR

Like a nosebleed, watery blood or clear fluid from the ear may be a sign of a fractured base of the skull if it happens after a head injury. However, it is usually due to local causes – often a hairgrip or other foreign body has been inserted into the ear and has perforated the eardrum. Other causes of a perforated eardrum are loud explosions, blows to the head and, most commonly, an infection in the middle ear. The person will always have experienced severe ear pain when this happens, which will often be relieved once the drum perforates. Ear infections may need antibiotics.

Dressing wounds

Even minor wounds can become infected and cause real problems with the victim's health. However, most bites, grazes and cuts heal without too much trouble and are easily treated. It is important that you are aware of the type of wound sustained so that you can carry out the appropriate first aid. Some wounds, such as puncture wounds, are more likely to cause damage to the underlying tissues and organs, and really need professional assessment by medical personnel.

TYPES OF WOUND

There are two main types of wound: closed and open. Closed wounds are usually caused by a blunt object, and vary from a small bruise to serious internal organ damage. A bruise the size of the injured person's fist would cause substantial blood loss.

Open wounds range from surface abrasions to deep puncture wounds. A laceration is a wound with jagged edges, which may cause heavy bleeding. As the object causing the wound may be very dirty, the risk of subsequent infection is high. Incisions are clean-edged cuts, such as those caused by a knife or broken glass, and may be deep. The wound may look relatively harmless, but there can be considerable damage to underlying tendons, nerves, blood vessels and even organs. Deep incisions may be life-threatening,

THE BASICS OF BANDAGING

- Make the injured person comfortable and offer reassurance. Work in front of them and start on the injured side.
- Make sure the injured part is supported while you work on it.
- Apply the bandage with a firm and even pressure, neither too tight nor too loose.
- Tie reef knots or secure with tape. Ensure all loose ends are tucked away.
- Check the circulation beyond the bandage and check on any bleeding.

BASIC FIRST AID FOR MAJOR WOUNDS

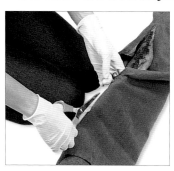

1 Expose the whole of the wound to assess the injury. Do not drag clothing over the wound, but cut or lift aside the clothing.

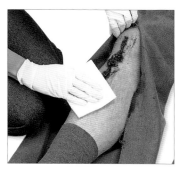

2 Using a gauze pad, clear the surface of the wound of any obvious debris such as large shards of glass, lumps of grit or mud.

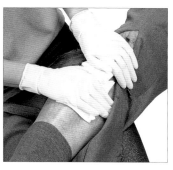

3 Control bleeding with direct pressure and then by elevating the limb.

4 Once bleeding is controlled, apply a bandage to the wound.

especially if the injury is around the chest or abdomen, and bleeding from incisions can take some time to stop.

Puncture wounds can be tricky to assess, as the size of the external wound gives no clue to how deep it goes (and the extent of tissue damage). Professional assessment may be needed.

All bites carry a high risk of infection, with human bites almost invariably becoming infected – a doctor should see any human bite at all, in case antibiotics are needed.

Guns can inflict many types of wound, and bleeding can be external and internal. Handguns, low-calibre rifles and shotguns fire fairly low-velocity projectiles, which usually stay in the body, while high-velocity bullets from military weapons often leave entry and exit wounds. High-velocity bullets create powerful shock waves throughout the body that can break bones and cause widespread damage.

The cutting or tearing off of body parts needs urgent help. Keep the severed part dry and cool and take it to hospital along with the person, as reattachment may be possible.

FIRST AID FOR MINOR WOUNDS

Avoid touching the wound, in order to prevent infection. Find out how and where the wound was caused. Wash it

BANDAGING A LIMB

1 Place the tail of the bandage below the injury and work from the inside to the outside, and from the furthermost part to the nearest.

2 Roll the bandage around the limb and start with two overlapping turns. Cover two-thirds of each turn with the new one. Finish with two overlapping turns.

3 Once you've finished, check the circulation; if the bandage is too tight, unroll it and reapply it slightly looser.

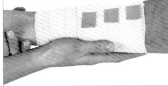

4 Secure the end with pieces of adhesive tape or tie the ends of the bandage using a reef knot.

under running water, or with bottled or boiled water. Dry the wound and apply a sterile adhesive dressing (plaster or Band-aid). For wounds that extend over a larger area, it may be better to use a non-adhesive dressing, sterile dressing and bandage. The wound must be kept clean and dry for the next few days.

A wound needs to stay fairly dry: wounds kept damp are more likely to become infected and can take longer to heal. If a dressing becomes wet, it should be changed for a dry one. Small wounds, grazes and blisters respond well to exposure to the air – provided dirt is unlikely to get into them.

INFECTED WOUNDS

Sometimes a wound becomes infected despite having been cleaned and dressed correctly. Some people are more vulnerable to infection, including those with diabetes, or with a compromised immune system.

You may notice the first signs of infection in and around a wound within hours, but it frequently takes longer to manifest itself. The infection may not surface until a day or two after the injury. Pain, redness, tenderness and swelling are all signs of infection. The person may also experience fever and notice pus oozing from the wound.

Infection may spread under the skin (cellulitis) and/or into the bloodstream (septicaemia). Suspect cellulitis if there is redness and swelling beyond the wound site. The glands in the armpits, neck or groins may be tender, and there may be a red line going up the limb towards the glands. Suspect septicaemia if the person feels unwell, with a fever, thirst, shivering and lethargy. These conditions require medical treatment. Tetanus can contaminate the tiniest of wounds, so immunization must be kept up to date.

Cover an infected wound with a sterile bandage. Leave the surrounding area visible, so that you can monitor signs of spreading infection. Elevate and support the area if possible and get medical help for the injured person as soon as possible.

DRESSING A WOUND WITH AN EMBEDDED OBJECT

1 Do not try to remove this kind of embedded object as you may cause further damage. Your aim is to deal with bleeding and protect the area from infection, and to get aid promptly.

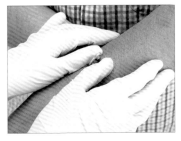

2 If the wound is bleeding, apply pressure to the surrounding area with your hands. Never apply pressure directly on to an embedded object. Elevating the wounded part will also help.

3 Place padding around the object. If possible, as it would be here, build this padding up until it is as high as the embedded object, ready to bandage over smoothly.

Bone Fractures

In the short term, the various methods used to deal with fractures focus on preventing the fracture from becoming worse. This is all you can hope to achieve if you find yourself in a remote area, until medical professionals can be summoned. The general idea is to immobilize the fracture and the joints above and below it, and this can be done either by cradling the affected limb or by surrounding it with padding.

Moving a fracture can cause severe pain, as well as damage to surrounding tissue and structures, and possibly further complications, such as shock, from bleeding or from bone penetrating through skin, nerves or blood vessels. Before dealing with a fracture, check that there are no other injuries that require more immediate treatment.

HAND OR ARM IMMOBILIZATION
This can be used on a fracture to the normally rigid bone of the hand or arm. Use your own hands and arms to cradle the injured limb in order to stop all movement. This method is most appropriate when medical help is expected to arrive fairly quickly, or when no other equipment or first aid materials of any kind are available.

If you are dealing with a simple fracture to an arm, and you are confident that bending the limb will not cause further damage, it will be more secure and convenient to put the arm in a broad arm sling in order to prevent movement, rather than to hold it. Use the sling in your first aid kit.

USING PADDING AND BOXES
These props are used mostly for leg fractures, though they are also suitable for arm fractures when bending the elbow to put the arm in a sling would cause further damage.

For this method, hold the fractured limb still, then roll large, loose sausage shapes from sweaters, towels or blankets, and place gently against the limb. Fill any gaps beneath the limb, such as from a bent knee, with just enough padding material to provide support without moving the limb at all. Finally, place books, boxes or other heavy items on either side of the limb to hold the padding in place.

This method is ideal if you can leave the injured person where they are until medical help arrives because it frees you as the first aider to concentrate on taking care of them.

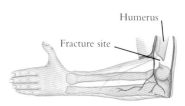

▲ *Fractures of the humerus above the elbow are common in children, whereas adults are more likely to fracture the shoulder end of this bone.*

SYMPTOMS OF A FRACTURE

- The injured person may have a visible history of impact or trauma at the fracture site.
- Bone may be penetrating the skin.
- Swelling, bruising or deformity may be visible at the fracture site. These may worsen over time.
- The person may feel pain on moving the limb.
- The person may feel numbness or tingling in the injured area.
- There may be additional wounds at or near the fracture site.
- The person may have heard the bones crack or grate against one another at the time of impact.

APPLYING A SLING FOR A SIMPLE ARM FRACTURE

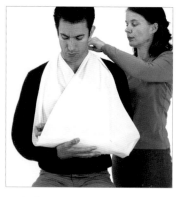

1 Ask the person to keep the arm still. Support the fracture and apply light padding, such as folded bubble wrap or a small towel (nothing too bulky).

2 The fracture should be immobilized completely. Apply a broad arm sling as shown, keeping the light padding in place within the sling.

3 Tie a second bandage across the chest to stabilize the sling and prevent movement while the person is in transit to hospital. Seek medical help.

COMMON FRACTURE TYPES

Simple or closed fracture
There is a clean break in the bone, with no displacement of the bone and no penetration of the skin.

Compound or open fractures
The broken ends of the bone stick out through the skin. The chance of infection is much higher.

Greenstick fracture
The fracture is on only one side of the bone, and the unbroken side bends over like a pliable young tree branch. This type of fracture is common in children.

Comminuted fracture
The bone is splintered at the fracture site, and smaller fragments of bone are found between two main fragments.

Fracture dislocation
The bone breaks or cracks near an already dislocated joint.

Avulsion fracture
A ligament or muscle attached to a bone has ripped off, taking a piece of the bone with it.

SPLINTS
Rigid supports for fractures are rarely used by medical professionals today, but they are useful if you are in a remote location when an accident occurs, and may have a long wait for professional help, or are forced to move the patient to reach a safe area. Improvised examples of splints include broom and shovel handles, or even sturdy, stripped tree branches. Add extra padding around the limb, using sweaters or towels, and fix the padding in place with tied bandages, scarves, rope or whatever equivalent you have available. As always with a fracture, your aim is to keep movement to an absolute minimum.

COMPOUND FRACTURES
When dealing with a compound or open fracture, it is important to prevent blood loss and reduce the chance of infection at the fracture site, as well as immobilizing the injured area. Seek

medical help or contact the emergency services urgently, if you can. While you wait, place a clean dressing or sterile pad over the wound site and apply hard pressure with your hands to either side of the protruding bone to control the bleeding. Do not press on the protruding bone.

Build up padding alongside the bone sticking out of the skin, and secure the dressing and padding with a bandage, but do not do so if it causes any movement of the limb and never bandage tightly. Monitor the person's condition as there is a risk of shock.

If you are forced to move the injured person, you may have to splint the fracture. Add extra padding around the limb and fix in place with tied bandages. Try to keep all movement to an absolute minimum.

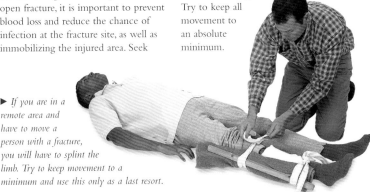

▶ *If you are in a remote area and have to move a person with a fracture, you will have to splint the limb. Try to keep movement to a minimum and use this only as a last resort.*

USING PADDING TO SUPPORT A LOWER LEG FRACTURE

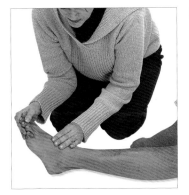

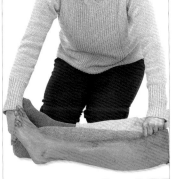

1 Help the person to lie down, then contact the emergency services. Feel the foot and lower leg for warmth and to check the person senses your touch.

2 Place soft padding in the middle of both legs, extending it well above the knee. The foot should be supported in the position in which it was found.

3 If you are forced to move the person yourself, secure the padding in place with bandages, placed well above and below the site of the fracture.

Chemical, electrical and inhalation burns

Chemical and electrical burns are especially hazardous, as further injury is possible both for casualty and helper. With a chemical incident, make the area safe or remove the casualty to safety and then get someone to inform the fire service about the chemical in question. Electrical burns can look deceptively mild at skin level while underlying muscles, nerves and organs may be badly burned. With both chemical and electrical burns, the casualty could go into shock, so monitor their vital signs until medical help arrives.

BURNS FROM CHEMICALS

Corrosive chemicals will continue to damage the skin while in contact with it so dispersing the harmful chemical as soon as possible is a priority. Chemical burns tend to develop more slowly than those from other causes. They may also

be particularly hazardous to the first-aider (because you may easily become burnt yourself) and they may give off fumes that could be inhaled. If there is any doubt about the chemical, move everyone away from the casualty and summon expert help.

You may recognize a burn as a chemical burn because:
• The casualty informs you what happened.
• There are containers of chemicals nearby.
• The casualty is suffering intense, stinging pain around the burnt area.
• After some time, blistering and discoloration may develop, along with swollen tissues in the affected area.

▼ *While wearing protective gloves, flood the burnt area with cold water to cool the skin and disperse the chemical.*

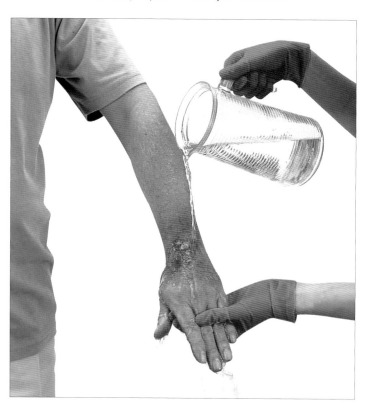

FIRST AID FOR CHEMICAL BURNS

Phone the emergency services or arrange urgent transport to hospital.

Get the casualty out of the contaminated area as soon as possible, without exposing yourself to danger.

Protect yourself. Wear appropriate gloves/apron if readily available; open windows and doors for ventilation.

Flood the injured part with water, for at least 10–15 minutes or until help arrives. Pour the water so that contaminated water neither runs on to other parts of the casualty's body nor on to you.

Remove any contaminated clothing, unless it is stuck fast to the skin.

WARNING

Do not try to "neutralize" the chemical (by putting alkali on acid or vice versa) as the resulting reaction may produce heat or could exacerbate the existing burn.

COMMON CAUSES OF CHEMICAL BURNS

Certain chemicals can irritate, burn or even penetrate the skin's protective layer. Many chemical-related accidents are in industry but the following are all household chemicals that are corrosive:
• Dishwasher products
• Oven cleaners
• Bleach
• Ammonia
• Caustic soda.

BURNS FROM ELECTRICITY

Electrical burns can occur from all kinds of electric current – from lightning strikes and overhead power cables to domestic current. There are three distinct types of electrical burn:
• A flash burn, caused by electricity arcing over a distance, and which leaves a distinctive residue on the skin that is sometimes coppery in appearance.
• Burns from flames caused by electricity.
• Direct burning of the tissues by an electric current.

ELECTRICITY-RELATED DAMAGE

Electrical burns can look deceptively mild. Like chemical burns, the extent of the burn may not be immediately obvious and often looks quite innocuous. There may be entry and exit wounds, which give an idea of the path of the electric current, but these are often hard to find.

Underneath the fairly normal-looking skin, the muscle, blood vessels and nerves may have literally "fried". What's more, the jolt of electricity could have affected the casualty's heartbeat.

If you arrive at an accident scene and find that the casualty is unconscious, first ensure they are not still connected to a live power source, and then check their airway, breathing and circulation (ABC) and be prepared to start resuscitation techniques immediately and to continue until emergency medical assistance arrives.

FIRST AID FOR ELECTRICAL BURNS

Do not touch the casualty unless and until you know they are no longer connected to a live electrical source.

If the casualty is unconscious, check their ABC and start resuscitation if necessary. Call the emergency services.

Treat as for a dry burn.

Watch for any signs of shock, or for any effects on the heartbeat. Note: Anyone who has suffered more than a mild tingling sensation should be seen at hospital – electricity can affect the heart some time after the initial exposure.

INHALATION BURNS

Breathing in dangerous fumes may affect the respiratory system – the trachea (windpipe), bronchi and lung tissue – and can cause serious damage. Such fumes include car exhaust emissions (including carbon monoxide), smoke from a fire, fumes from faulty domestic appliances (such as a gas heater) and fumes from smouldering foam-filled upholstered furniture. Certain chemicals, including dry-cleaning solvents, may also give off toxic or irritant fumes.

Signs of inhalation burns:
• Soot and singed hairs around the mouth and nose area.
• Breathing difficulties.
• Headache.
• Dizziness.
• Shock.

The best first-aid approach is as follows: Send for the emergency services; get the casualty to a safe place in clean air and do not expose yourself to fire, smoke or fumes; position the casualty sitting up and supported; monitor the casualty for changes in consciousness or breathing; be prepared to resuscitate if necessary (however, if chemicals have been inhaled, then this may be unsafe without special equipment).

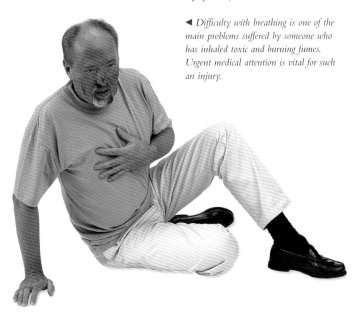

◄ *Difficulty with breathing is one of the main problems suffered by someone who has inhaled toxic and burning fumes. Urgent medical attention is vital for such an injury.*

Understanding poisoning

The golden rule in giving first aid for a suspected poisoning is never to attempt to make the casualty vomit until you know what the poison is. Vomiting a poisonous substance back up the oesophagus (gullet) can double the damage if the poison is a corrosive chemical. Poisons can get into the body in many ways – via the skin, digestive system, lungs or bloodstream. The mode of entry influences the speed of reaction; for instance if a poison is injected into the bloodstream, it can reach all parts of the body within a minute or so.

A poison is any substance that can cause temporary or permanent damage to the body if taken in sufficient quantities. Poisoning may occur accidentally or intentionally. Suicide attempts often involve more than one poisonous agent, and the casualty may resist any help that is offered. Some drugs have no obvious immediate effects when taken in overdose but ultimately are fatal.

Accidental poisoning is most often seen in children and in the elderly. There are fewer deaths from such incidents in children, but some agents may wreak havoc in a child. Elderly people may get confused and take the wrong medicine or the wrong dosage.

There are a wide variety of common poisons:
• Noxious gases or fumes.
• Cleaning products.
• Toxins in plants and fungi.
• Bacterial and viral toxins (in food).
• Drugs and alcohol.
• Toxins from bites and stings.

▶ *If a person is unconscious, place them in the recovery position and keep a close eye on them until the emergency services arrive.*

Assess the casualty's ABC (airway, breathing and circulation). If they are breathing but unconscious, put them in the recovery position.

If they are not breathing, start resuscitation techniques once you have checked that there is no poison on the face or in the mouth area.

Phone or get someone to phone the emergency services.

If they start to have a fit, do not restrain them. Keep them out of danger and ensure a clear airway.

Look around to see if you can find any clues to the identity of the poison that has been taken. If the casualty has vomited, take a sample of the vomit to hospital as there is a good chance it will help doctors identify the appropriate treatment.

IDENTIFYING THE CAUSE OF THE POISONING

Once you have dealt with the casualty's immediate needs, gather information to try to identify the poison:
• Look for empty pill bottles or loose pills on the floor. Bag them and give to the emergency services.
• Search for codes on containers that will identify any chemical.
• Scan the area for a dead insect or snake to bag up and take to hospital.
• Cast your eye around for any potentially poisonous foods.

Alcohol and illicit drugs

In moderate amounts, alcohol is easily detoxified by the liver; but in very large quantities alcohol becomes a poison that the body can no longer deal with – and it can prove fatal. The same doesn't go, however, for many illicit drugs. Even small amounts of a substance such as cocaine or fumes from glue can result in severe effects on the body. Emergency medical treatment is vital, especially if a child has taken alcohol or a drug because children absorb the toxins much more quickly than adults.

ALCOHOL POISONING

Risks related to alcohol include:
• Depression of the central nervous system, most seriously the brain.
• Widening of blood vessels, risking loss of body heat and hypothermia.
• The inebriated person may choke on their vomit while unconscious.

SYMPTOMS OF ALCHOHOL INTOXICATION

• A smell of alcohol on the breath.
• Flushed and warm skin.
• Bottles or cans nearby.
• Actions are aggressive or passive.
• Speech and actions are slow and become less coordinated.
• Deep, noisy breathing.
• Low level of consciousness; they may pass in and out of consciousness.

If you suspect alcohol abuse or poisoning:
• Check that the casualty is rousable by shaking them and shouting their name.
• Move them into the recovery position and try to keep them there.
• Phone the emergency services and do not leave them until the ambulance arrives. If they regain consciousness meanwhile, you could give them some water to drink.

SOLVENT ABUSE

Children and adolescents are the main solvent abusers – they may inhale fumes from glue, paint, lighter fuel, cleaning fluids, aerosols and nail polish to "get high". All such solvents depress breathing and heart activity, and may cause respiratory and cardiac arrest.

FIRST AID FOR SOLVENT ABUSE POISONING

If the casualty's breathing or heart beat has stopped, start resuscitation immediately.

If unconscious but their ABC (airway, breathing and circulation) is normal, place them in the fresh air in the recovery position.

Phone the emergency services.

Check their ABC regularly.

Often, the casualty starts to "come round" quickly and may seem normal after 20 minutes. Stay with them until help arrives.

ILLICIT DRUGS

Illicit stimulant drugs include Ecstasy, cocaine, amphetamines and LSD. If you suspect someone has taken any of these drugs, watch out for the following signs:
• Excitable and hyperactive behaviour.
• Sweating.
• Shaking hands.
• Hallucinations.
These drugs can occasionally be fatal. Ecstasy interferes with the brain's ability to control body temperature, which can rise to over 42°C (107.6°F) and cause heat exhaustion. Ecstasy-takers often drink lots of water, which can cause kidney malfunction and abnormal heart rhythms. Cocaine's main effects are on the heart rate – with the potential to lead to abnormal rhythms and even cardiac arrest.

Opiate drugs such as heroin and codeine may depress the respiratory system, causing breathing to stop. Rapid recovery occurs if a particular drug is given intravenously, but this must be done urgently, by medical personnel.

FIRST AID FOR ILLICIT DRUG POISONING

Do not try to make the casualty vomit.

Place them in the recovery position.

Phone the emergency services.

Check their ABC and monitor their breathing every 10 minutes.

◄ *Children and teenagers are the main abusers of solvents. When dealing with a casualty, it is vital to maintain their breathing and circulation and get them to hospital as soon as possible.*

Survival resources and Acknowledgements

PUBLICATIONS

The following books are recommended for further reading:
• *Streetwise* (Peter Consterdine, Protection Publications)
• *Stopping Rape – Successful Survival Strategies* (Pauline Bart and Patricia O'Brien, Pergamon Press)
• *Principles of Personal Defense* (Jeff Cooper, Paladin Press)
• *Justifiable Force: The Practical Guide to the Law of Self Defence* (Robert Manning, Barry Rose Law Publishers)
• *US Armed Forces Survival Manual* (edited by John Boswell, Corgi)
• *SAS Survival Handbook* and *The Urban Survival Handbook* (Lofty Wiseman, HarperCollins)
• *The Worst-Case Scenario Survival Handbook* (Piven & Borgenicht, Chronicle Books)
• *The Book of Survival* (Anthony Greenbank, Hatherleigh Press)
• *The Encyclopedia of Outdoor Survival* (Barry Davies, Virgin Books)
• *Combat And Survival Magazine* (Mai Publications, editor Bob Morrison, www.combatandsurvival.com)

WEBSITES

The contributors recommend the following survival, self-defence and government travel advisory sites:
www.activekids.com
Gives information on martial art clubs around the country

www.real-self-defense.com
Self-defence tips
www.thecombatgroup.com
Self-defence, martial arts, personal security and travel security books, dvds and courses
www.smartraveller.gov.au
The Australian Government's travel advisory and consular assistance service
www.publicsafety.gc.ca
Official Canadian homeland security site
www.govt.nz
New Zealand government's official site
www.security.co.za
Definitive site on security in South Africa, with good links.
www.dhs.gov
Official US homeland security and disasters and emergencies website
www.ukpreppersguide.co.uk
UK-based site on preparing against disasters
www.survive.co.uk
UK-based site on how to survive emergencies
www.theprepared.com
US-based site on preparing against disasters

SELF-DEFENCE COURSES

• Combat Academy
www.combat-academy.co.uk
• Muay Thai Boxing links website
www.ukmtf.com
• British Combat Association
www.britishcombat.co.uk
• Krav Maga
www.kravmaga.com
• Free online self-defence courses
www.womensselfdefence_seps.com

ACKNOWLEDGEMENTS

The publishers and contributors wish to thank the following people for their time, expertise and contributions to the book. We sincerely apologize if we have omitted any individual(s).
Debra Searle (Veal) MBE and her sister Hayley Barnard at SHOAL Projects Ltd for providing photographs for the introduction.
www.debrasearle.com
Bill Mattos for photography, modelling and for providing many of the props.
Kiah Allen for photography and modelling.

Yazmin Dunne for author photograph.
John Campbell and Jay Francey for modelling.
Tim Gundry for shooting the self-defense sequences:
www.timgundry.com
Mr and Mrs Turner at Kazan Budo Ltd (Martial Arts supplies) and Bellingham Fitness Centre for supplying the gym, models, props and lunches for the self-defence sequences.
Bob Morrison's Military Scene for the military and biological pictures
www.combatandsurvival.com
Patrick Mulrey for his invaluable survival step-by-steps and disaster scenario illustrations.
Sheila Cook and the members of the Hexham Seijinkai Karate-do Club for modelling: Katie Khudarieh, Katy Cook, Sheila Cook, Catriona Moreland, Malcolm Wilson, Lucy Anne Donnelly.

With thanks to the following picture agencies for the photographs they provided:
iStockphoto: p2, p96tr, p99bl, p65tr, p70bl, p72bl, p77tl, p106tr, p114tr, p114bt, p118bl, p119tr, p120–21, p125tr, p127tl, p128tl, p130tr.
Sciencephoto Library: p116tr, p124bl, p125ml, mr, bl, bt, p126bl, p122.
Alamy Images: p72tr, p76tr, p107tr, p113tl, p120tr.
Shutterstock: p7t, p10t, br, p11b, p12, p13bl, br, p14–15, p19 (both), p29b, p45br, p46b, p50t, p103bl, p128b, p129t, 131 (both), p132 (both).

Index

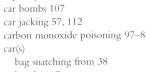

ABOUT THE AUTHOR

Bill Mattos has written numerous books and hundreds of magazine articles, mostly on outdoor adventure related matters. His adventures have taken him all over the world, in mountains from Norway to the Italian Alps, from the Pacific Islands to the North Sea, and more airports than he cares to remember.

He's lived on his wits fishing and skinning rabbits in Wales, and camped for a month in a bivvy bag in Canada. Bill has trained with many kinds of firearms, from handguns through shotguns to rifles and AR's, and is proficient in the martial arts including Judo and Kung Fu.

Bill has worked as an engineer, rigger, designer, stuntman, photographer and videographer, all providing varied input and inspiration for his first love of writing. Bill currently lives in Cornwall. For more information see www.billmattos.com